A SAND COUNTY ALMANAC

With Essays on Conservation

"There are some who can live without wild things, and some who cannot. These essays are the delights and dilemmas of one who cannot."

Aldo Leopold

A SAND COUNTY

Photographs by Michael Sewell   Introduction by Kenneth Brower

...arious

...pold

...ccording to the County Clerk, is the extent

...ty Clerk is a sleepy fellow, who never

what they would show at daybreak

...tent — both to my dog and myself,

...ner of all the acres I can walk

...supposed to exist in my county,

...ch. How far that is, I've never been

...have tenants. They are negligent

...about tenures. Indeed at every

ALMANAC

With Essays on Conservation

Oxford University Press   New York

OXFORD
UNIVERSITY PRESS

Oxford   New York

Athens Auckland Bangkok Bogotá Buenos Aires Cape Town Chennai Dar es Salaam
Delhi Florence Hong Kong Istanbul Karachi Kolkata Kuala Lumpur Madrid
Melbourne Mexico City Mumbai Nairobi Paris São Paulo Shanghai Singapore
Taipei Tokyo Toronto Warsaw

and associated companies in

Berlin Ibadan

Copyright © 1949 by Oxford University Press, Inc.
Photographs © 2001 by Michael Sewell
Introduction © 2001 by Kenneth Brower

Published by Oxford University Press, Inc., 198 Madison Avenue, New York, New York 10016

Oxford is a registered trademark of Oxford University Press.

Library of Congress Cataloging-in-Publication Data

Leopold, Aldo, 1886-1948.
     A sand county almanac : with essays on conservation / Aldo Leopold ; photographs by
     Michael Sewell : introduction by Kenneth Brower.--New ed.
          p. cm.
     ISBN 0-19-514617-4
     1. Natural history--Outdoor books. 2. Natural history--United States. 3. Nature
     conservation--United States. I. Title.

QH81.L56 2001
508.73--dc21   2001034038

1 3 5 7 9 8 6 4 2

This illustrated edition of *A Sand County Almanac* was produced by Michael and Denise Sewell
and Kenneth Brower at Visual Pursuit Design in Forest Knolls, California, in conjunction with
Oxford University Press. Editing by Kenneth Brower and Michael Sewell.

Design and production by Denise Sewell

Jacket photograph (front): the Shack in autumn; (back): lily pads in October © Michael Sewell
Endpapers: Sand County manuscript © Dept. of Special Collections, Univ. of Wisconsin-Madison
Title page photograph: sandhill cranes in flight © Michael Sewell
Introduction photographs: the Shack circa 1936; Daughter Estella on the farm gate circa 1937 © A. Carl Leopold
Foreword photograph: Aldo Leopold, 1947 © Charles C. Bradley

Printed in Hong Kong on acid-free paper

To my Estella

CONTENTS

Introduction

THE SHACK SITS JUST ABOVE A SANDY FLOOD CHANNEL OF THE WISCONSIN RIVER, at a fork in the evolution of our regard for the land. The windows—salvage glass, white-shuttered in dark-weathered walls—look out on a landscape formed toward the close of the Wisconsin, the last ice age, when the sand of the "sand counties" was laid down in vast alluvial deposits. In one cataclysmic glacial outburst flood, 500 feet of sand were heaped up in places in just days, forcing the Wisconsin to change course.

Just beyond the Shack's woodpile, a low ridge rises—an old glacial moraine forested now with volunteer maples and transplanted pines. A short distance up the moraine, sunk in the golden leaf litter of the maples, is a pit lined by rounded stones. This was the basement of the man Aldo Leopold called ". . . our predecessor the bootlegger, who hated this farm, skinned it of residual fertility, burned its farmhouse, threw it back into the lap of the County (with delinquent taxes to boot), and then disappeared among the landless anonymities of the Great Depression."

The pines growing everywhere on Leopold's 120 acres are living monuments to his experiments with restoration, to his ideas on stewardship. The pit of the bootlegger's basement is monument to our landowning ethic before Aldo came.

If the environmental movement has sacred texts—literary cornerstones—then they are Thoreau's *Walden*, George Perkins Marsh's *Man and Nature*, Carson's *Silent Spring*, and Leopold's *A Sand County Almanac*. The almanac is an epochal, seminal, ageless work. It is bible still for land managers; koran for those of us who work the soil where literature overlaps ecology; urtext for the ecological restoration movement.

The beginnings of ecological restoration—the first systematic attempt to reassemble disturbed ecosystems—came in 1934, when the University of Wisconsin at Madison, under Leopold's leadership, set out to build a collection of native ecological communities on abandoned farmland. (Aldo's ruined farm, bought the next year as a week-end retreat, became homework in this endeavor.) The University's Arboretum restored thirty distinct systems, all the important plant communities native to the upper Midwest.

The view from the Shack was provident and clear. Leopold understood before anyone that the century or two of the Preservation Era will prove to be prologue, an introductory chapter, noble but brief. Almost all the wilderness that can be saved has been saved. For the duration of our time on the planet—for whatever piece of eternity we have left here—restoration will be the great task.

Prairie smoke in spring

In October 1999, the fiftieth anniversary of *Sand County's* publication, photographer Michael Sewell and I took up residence in the Shack. We made ourselves comfortable there at the epicenter of modern environmentalism. Tossing our things on bunks in the sleeping alcove, we poked around.

I checked the guestbook for the impressions of previous visitors. Like guestbooks everywhere, this one was an epic of numbing banality. "Although difficult to express through the written word, I must say my thoughts regarding this place are of high esteem." And so on. Michael Sewell peeked in a cigar box on a shelf, then brought it over and placed it reverentially in my hands. Inside were Aldo Leopold's bird bands, his banding pliers, and an old envelope of "Aldo Leopold" stationary, penciled with bird lists in his handwriting.

Sitting in front of the Shack, that first morning, I reacquainted myself with *Sand County.* I had not read the book cover to cover since my teens. I was struck immediately by Leopold's debt to Thoreau—too great a debt, one might have said. Leopold is Thoreau's direct descendent in a literary and philosophical way. Aldo's genius is not the extraterrestrial sort of genius you see in Thoreau, who seemed to have no antecedents. It is warmer and more down to earth. Whenever I found a riff that seemed a little too Thoreauvian, I flagged it in pencil in Leopold's margins. Leopold, who was a bit of a dandy in his dress, sometimes got a little fancy in his prose. He had a fondness for locutions that were archaic even in the '40s. "I would I were a muskrat" or "ready, nay eager. . ." I dutifully flagged each of these infractions in his margins.

Then, somewhere in the "If I Were the Wind" section, I realized I was hearing no more echos of Thoreau. Leopold had found his own voice. Or perhaps it was *I* who had found Leopold's voice.

At the core of Thoreau there is something feverish. At the core of Leopold there is a calm. Leopold is a species of man now nearly extinct: a tranquil generalist who immersed himself in place. We no longer have any writer, thinker, who is so attentive to the details of natural history and natural locality, so comfortable with the passage of time. What shines through *Sand County* is an unconditional love for this farm and for the American land.

For a week Sewell and I followed after Aldo, wandering all over the Leopold farm. We found beaver-felled trees above the great marsh. We flushed wild turkeys from the margins of the Levee Road. In the interior "uplands," as the locals like to call these imperceptible elevations, we surprised white-tailed deer. The river, we found, was the place for vistas—and for kingfishers, killdeer, cormorants. A juvenile bald eagle watched us daily from its favorite snag on the far shore.

This was the first of several trips that Sewell would take to Wisconsin. As my copy of *Sand County* filled with marginalia—all of it now appreciative—the margins of

Sewell's copy filled with ideas on how to illustrate this text. He had set himself limits: He would not stray from Leopold's footsteps. His photography for this book would be confined to the farm and surrounding countryside. The photographer's copy of the book was soon dog-eared. It would end up in tatters.

Sewell set up his remote camera downhill from the Shack, aiming the infrared beam of the trigger low across the trail that edged the slough. We collected feral apples, dumped them in the vicinity of the beam, and crushed them underfoot. For good measure, Sewell sprayed apple-juice from an atomizer on surrounding boughs and twigs. In the morning, all the apples were gone, and frames 14-27 of the roll had been exposed—self-portraits of deer, it turned out. At dusk we labored, stung by nettles and mosquitos, to set up Sewell's camera blind on a small pond in the great marsh. By morning light, the photographer, peering out, found the water wall-to-wall in geese.

The Wisconsin flows past the Leopold farm nearly as dark and tannic as the Rio Negro. Every evening, a half-hour before sunset, I would walk to the river to watch the evening flight of sandhill cranes to their roosting beaches on the far shore. They passed overhead in synchronized duos, threesomes, and squadrons, honking the chortling, contrapuntal honk of cranes.

In 1935, when Leopold bought his farm, there were only 25 nesting pairs of sandhill cranes in Wisconsin. The species became one of his special concerns. "The ultimate value in these marshes is wildness, and the crane is wildness incarnate," he wrote. He corresponded with anyone in the state who knew anything of sandhill cranes: the landowner who had a breeding pair on his property, the Department of Natural Resources employee who had glimpsed one of the birds. His efforts, and those of his colleagues, paid off. Today there are 12,000 sandhill cranes in Wisconsin. Nothing would have cheered Leopold more. Restoration works. On the road to extinction, traffic travels both ways.

Otter Pond had no otter during Aldo's tenure. The last specimen of *Lutra canadensis* was extirpated before he came. Late in the 1990s, *Lutra canadensis* recolonized, and there are otter again in Otter Pond. Radio-collared wolves now occasionally pass through, as well. No one has seen wolves on Leopold land, as yet, but their signals have betrayed them.

If there is a pivotal moment in Aldo Leopold's life, as revealed in *A Sand County Almanac and Sketches Here and There*, it is in his account of his shooting of an Arizona wolf: "We reached the old wolf in time to watch a fierce green fire dying in her eyes. I realized then, and have known ever since, that there was something new to me in those eyes—something known only to her and to the mountain."

That fierce green fire glows again in the sand counties of Wisconsin.

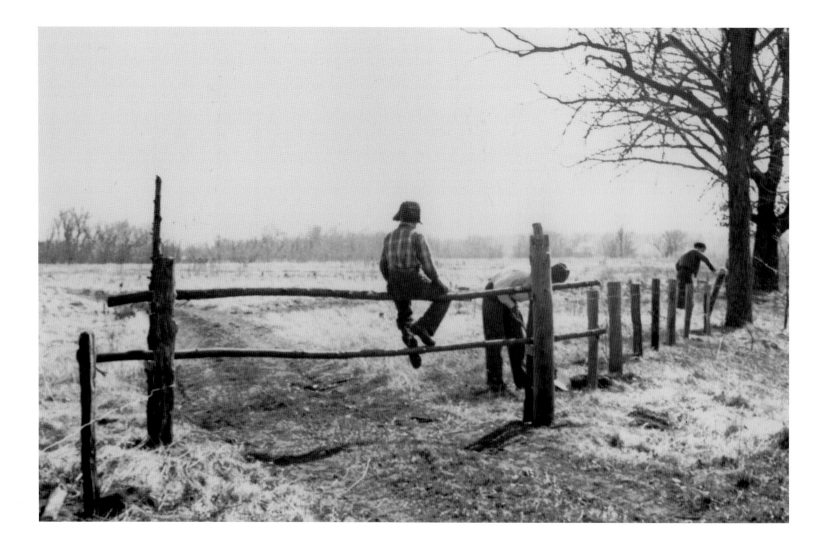

Wellington B. Huffaker IV led me along the moraine, down the trail to the good oak. Huffaker is a cherubic, bearded, thirtyish man who employs his full name mainly as a joke and goes by "Buddy." Formerly the ecologist for the Aldo Leopold Foundation, he had just been appointed executive director. "The job came ten years too early," he confessed of his promotion. "I wanted more dirt under my fingernails." It was the timeless complaint of the forester, the field archaeologist, the back-country ranger. The outdoors is what draws these people in, but advancement means a desk. Leopold himself was brilliant in balancing the two, but this seems to have grown more difficult for the generations after him.

We reached the good oak, or the site where that famous tree had stood. The "Good Oak" section of *Sand County's* February chapter, and its account of the felling of that tree, is the first tour de force of the book. Leopold's crosscut saw, piling up "fragrant little chips of history," cuts back through seventy years of growth rings: the 1930s, the era of the bootlegger; 1924, the death of Wisconsin's last marten; 1908, the last cougar in Wisconsin. The oak beautifully encapsulates the history of land mismanagement in Wisconsin and the nation.

"Nina always says her father got the most out of a really insignificant tree," said Buddy, gazing at the spot.

Nina Leopold Bradley, Aldo's older daughter, was right. From the good oak her father had got firewood, exercise, family teamwork, and a history lesson. Her observation, it struck me, was synecdochical. It applied by extension to the whole Leopold spread. Her father had got the most from a really insignificant farm, and in his success at this, the farm, like the oak, has gained enormous significance.

Huffaker led me on down the moraine. The gentle elevations of this feature, called "the Clay Hill" on the south side and "the Sand Hill" on the north, makes the spine of the Leopold property and the only real topography on it. We stopped at the spot that inspired Leopold's short ode to the tiny plant Draba.

"Draba plucks no heartstrings," goes the fourth and final paragraph. "Its perfume, if there is any, is lost in the gusty winds. Its color is plain white. Its leaves wear a sensible woolly coat. Nothing eats it; it is too small. No poets sing of it. Some botanist once gave it a Latin name, and then forgot it. Altogether it is of no importance—just a small creature that does a small job quickly and well."

Daughter Estella on the farm gate circa 1937; the same spot today

The best Leopold prose is like this: clear and plain, yet with an accent of idiosyncratic language and an undercurrent of private belief (his use here of "creature" to include vegetation—as if plants too had spirits). The theme is pure Leopold: an insignificant plant leveraged, by his pen, into significance.

"There was a sand blow here," Buddy said. "But the microclimate has changed. We haven't been able to find Draba here for four years. We do find it down by the river. It's in the Lobelia family. It likes it really hot and dry. Leopold avoided planting pines in this area in order to maintain the sand blow. But they encroached anyway."

Leopold's prolific pines stretched away in all directions.

"Acts of creation are ordinarily reserved for gods and poets, but humbler folk may circumvent this restriction if they know how," Leopold wrote in *Sand County*. "To plant a pine, for example, one need be neither god nor poet; one need only own a shovel. By virtue of this curious loophole in the rules, any clodhopper may say: Let there be a tree—and there will be one.

"If his back be strong and his shovel sharp, there may eventually be ten thousand. And in the seventh year he may lean upon his shovel, and look upon his trees, and find them good."

Leopold was too modest. He had planted far more than 10,000 pines. He planted, truth be told, too many.

"He planted 48,000 pines in thirteen years here," Buddy Huffaker told me. "There's really way too many pines, compared to Wisconsin in pre-contact times."

I asked Huffaker if he had any intuitions about what Leopold, armed with today's information, would have done about his excess of pines.

"That's always the question," he answered. "Leopold was working with the best knowledge available at the time, the best information on ecological restoration, though they didn't call it that yet. The whole concept of community ecology was just emerging. It was brand-new stuff. Now we know that pine trees aren't as good a wildlife habitat as we once thought they were. It's certainly logical that he would say, 'Clearcut these trees, and let's put it to prairie and savanna.' *But it's not for him.* This place is for everyone who comes with a piece of his story that they want to understand better."

My own guess is that Leopold, with good humor and little regret, would have felled much of his forest, but I took Huffaker's point. The trees were almost irrelevant. What prospered in this sandy soil were not Leopold's pines so much as his ideas.

The Leopold Foundation collaborates with a neighboring outfit, the International Crane Foundation, in much of its prairie restoration. One October morning, on the path to a resurrected prairie on the ICF grounds at Baraboo, I joined several Leopold Foundation interns and a group of students from Germantown High School. We had come to harvest seed.

"We need seed! We got seed greed!" Jeb Barzen, Director of Field Ecology for the ICF, told the Germantown students. "We need forty bags of seed of Indian grass to plant ten acres. It's ridiculous how much seed we need."

Barzen told the kids that in the past twenty years students from Germantown High had raised $15,000 toward prairie restoration. "Since 1976, Germantown High has been working on this prairie," he said. "We call it the Germantown Prairie. Some of the prairie you see grew from seeds that your predecessors at Germantown High collected. Only ten percent of Wisconsin's original prairie is left. Your contribution will be measurable in terms of that prairie."

The International Crane Foundation is dedicated to the preservation of the world's fifteen species of crane and to the defense of crane habitat. The ICF runs a captive breeding center for endangered cranes in Baraboo and has embarked on Leopoldian restoration projects all over the world—in Keoladeo National Park in India, in the Han River estuary in Korea, in three provinces of China, in Muraviovka Park in Russia. The outfit had just launched an ambitious attempt to restore the Zambezi Delta. "In the Mekong Delta, we work in a wetland restoration project on the Plain of Reeds," Barzen told me. "About 15,000 acres. But we're also dealing with issues over the whole Mekong River, and we're working in Cambodia, trying to establish wetland areas there."

On reaching the Germantown Prairie, we scattered into the tall grass. "Don't collect that turkey foot," Barzan warned, of big bluestem. "Just this Indian grass. It's an early successional. These big aggressive grasses are important."

We watched the Germantown sophomores and juniors strip seed from their prairie.

"Leopold said that when it came right down to it, there were two things that interested him," Barzan said. "The relationship of people to the land, and the relationship of people to each other. This has everything to do with restoration. The ecology, relatively speaking is easy—it actually can mend itself—but because people are involved, that doesn't happen.

"I know exactly when I first read *Sand County.* I was in sixth grade when my dad gave it to me. I still remember getting teased by kids in my class. I was reading the essay on January thaw, very early in the *Almanac,* where he talks about pink rabbit urine. All the sixth grade boys thought this was pretty good joke. Pink rabbit urine. I didn't understand much about *A Sand County Almanac* then, but it had a huge influence on me. As it has any other time that I've read it.

"How many times have you read 'The Land Ethic,' say? Was it the same read every time? As you gain more perspective, more experience, you can understand the depth at which the book is written. With new experiences you understand greater depths. And that's the mark of any good literature, I think."

A FIFTIETH-ANNIVERSARY CONFERENCE, "Building on Leopold's Legacy: Conservation for a New Century," was concluding in Madison when I arrived in Wisconsin. As it neared time for me to leave, a new symposium, the 27th Annual Conference on South Asia, was beginning in the same hotel. My sister Barbara, a specialist in the Sherpas of Nepal, was attending this second meeting, and I drove into town for a visit. That evening in Leopold's town, surrounded by Himalayanists, I thought to inquire about Leopold's reputation in their country, up at the top of the world.

"Leopold is held up again and again by everyone in community forestry," a high-altitude forester named Mark Baker said. "The idea of stewardship. The idea that landowners are imbued with responsibilities to the land and to each other. That comes from Leopold." Paul Benjamin, a Wisconsin Department of Agriculture land-use planner with experience in Nepal, overheard. "We have too many deer in Wisconsin," he offered, playfully. "We have too many geese. And now we have wolves in Wisconsin. That's all Leopold's fault."

That Leopold should still inform scholars of the Himalaya, fifty years after his death, did not surprise me. I had encountered this Leopold Effect everywhere. At a

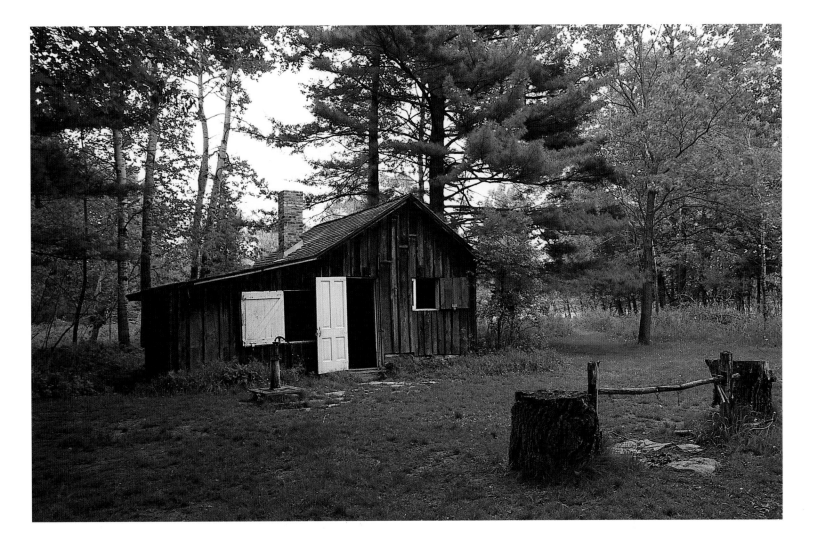

"restoration fair" in San Francisco, not long before, I had wandered the stalls asking about Leopold. Among a few of the youngest restorationists, the name drew a blank, but most of the activists in the exposition hall smiled at hearing it. They knew Leopold's place in the history of their movement. Even the disclaimers were illuminating. I asked a Scot named Featherstone, author of *Saving the Chaldonian Forest*, about Leopold's reputation in Scotland.

"I would think he has less influence in Britain than over here," Featherstone answered.

We debated whether Leopold's legacy was more in wilderness advocacy or in restoration. I argued for the latter. "Remember that Leopold line about the importance of saving all the parts," I said.

"'The First Law of Intelligent Tinkering,'" Featherstone quoted.

Perhaps it's true that the Scots are not much influenced by Leopold, but this particular Scot knew Leopold by heart.

The Shack circa 1936; the Shack today
Following page: autumn, Sedge Meadow

It's a game most pilgrims to the farm end up playing, I think: Where's Aldo?

For me, Aldo did not seem to be lingering much around the Shack. The cigar box on the shelf—the one containing his chickadee bands and handwritten bird notes—was certainly a reliquary of Aldo-ness. A renewable ghost of Leopold jumped out each time you opened the lid. Otherwise, the building did not move me. The Shack seemed just a shack. Mine was a minority opinion, I knew from the guestbook. "This is a holy place, and I think of it often as we fight today's battles to pass on our heritage," wrote Brock Evans of the Endangered Species Coalition. "I have often thought how wonderful it would be to come to this special place," wrote Mike Finley, superintendent of Yellowstone National Park. The Shack was Monticello, it was Lincoln's cabin, and yet somehow I was not awed.

Where I did find Aldo was outdoors.

Passing autumn blackberries, I would think "red lanterns," his metaphor for those scarlet leaves. Wading into the predawn mist on the great marsh, I sensed him very near. "Like the white ghost of a glacier," Aldo wrote of this mist, and this is exactly right. The field of mist is vaguely lenticular, like an ice sheet. The mist recalled the metaphor. It was as if Leopold and his dog had dematerialized in the fog just ahead.

But mostly Aldo was up in the Wisconsin sky.

He was certainly in formation with the cranes. He was in the crane honks and trumpeting, and in the steep glide angle of crane descent, and in the way the stilts of the legs drop and dangle when the bird is still a hundred feet above ground. He was in the fast, shifting skeins of Canada geese. In the evening, wedge after wedge passed over the peak of the Shack, then over the Leopold forest, headed across the river. When the geese passed high, what you heard was the circularity of their honking. They were singing a round. When the geese passed low, you heard the whoosh of the wingbeats, too, and a sibilance at the wingtips.

"Goose wings," I wrote in my notebook. "Not so much to escape enemies as to chase the seasons."

The line pleased me inordinately. Why, I wondered, had "chase the seasons" seemed so satisfactory? The effect was vaguely Aldoesque. Was that it? Was *Sand County* a standard I had internalized? I had faulted Aldo for his debt to Thoreau, but what about my debt to Aldo? To what extent had his rhythms and sensibilities become my own?

SO THAT'S WHERE ALDO WAS. He was both everywhere and no longer here. Traces of him lingered around the farm, but for the most part he had flown.

Of the migration of geese, he had written, ". . .the waste corn of Illinois is carried through the clouds to the Arctic tundras, there to combine with the waste sunlight of a nightless June to grow goslings for all the lands between." Something similar had happened to Aldo. He had dispersed. He was loose in the world combining with things. He was in my sentences, and in Mike Finley's directives on the management of Yellowstone's elk. He sat in on Jeb Barzen's negotiations with Chinese villagers. He subtly guided discussions that Jeb's colleague, Rich Beilfuss, held with villagers in Mozambique. He was silent partner in dozens of little businesses like Bluestem Farm, in Baraboo, which sells native wildflowers and grasses ("Nursery grown Wisconsin ecotypes available all seasons"). He resided chiefly now in our collective consciousness, that dimensionless yet vast geography that preceded cyberspace and dwarfs it still. His influence remained strong in various projects along the Wisconsin, and now he was busy along the Mekong, too. He was up in the rhododendron forests of the Himalaya. He was in Scotland's Chaldonian forest. He was out on the Zambezi Delta. He was down in the Plain of Reeds.

—*Kenneth Brower*

Oakland, California, April 21, 2001

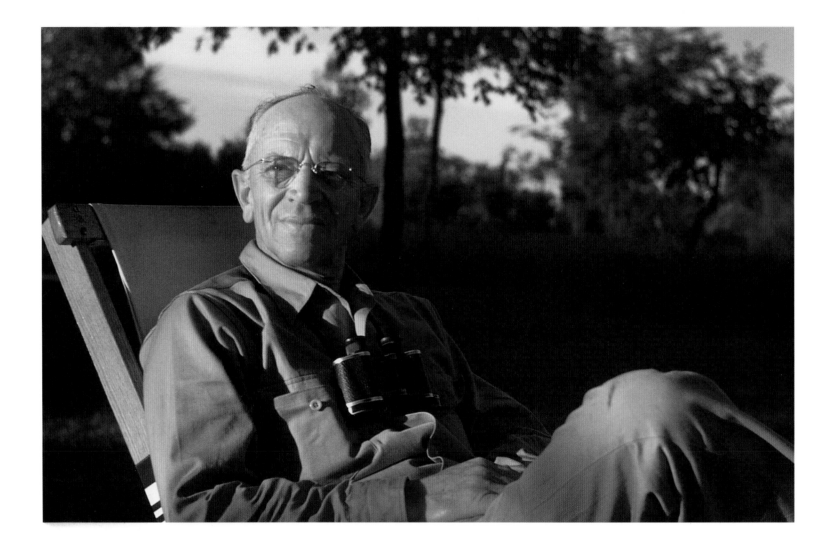

Foreword

THERE ARE SOME WHO CAN LIVE WITHOUT WILD THINGS, and some who cannot. These essays are the delights and dilemmas of one who cannot.

Like winds and sunsets, wild things were taken for granted until progress began to do away with them. Now we face the question whether a still higher 'standard of living' is worth its cost in things natural, wild, and free. For us of the minority, the opportunity to see geese is more important than television, and the chance to find a pasque-flower is a right as inalienable as free speech.

These wild things, I admit, had little human value until mechanization assured us of a good breakfast, and until science disclosed the drama of where they come from and how they live. The whole conflict thus boils down to a question of degree. We of the minority see a law of diminishing returns in progress; our opponents do not.

❧   ❧   ❧

CONSERVATION IS GETTING NOWHERE because it is incompatible with our Abrahamic concept of land. We abuse land because we regard it as a commodity belonging to us. When we see land as a community to which we belong, we may begin to use it with love and respect. There is no other way for land to survive the impact of mechanized man, nor for us to reap from it the esthetic harvest it is capable, under science, of contributing to culture.

That land is a community is the basic concept of ecology, but that land is to be loved and respected is an extension of ethics. That land yields a cultural harvest is a fact long known, but latterly often forgotten.

These essays attempt to weld these three concepts.

Such a view of land and people is, of course, subject to the blurs and distortions of personal experience and personal bias. But wherever the truth may lie, this much is crystal-clear: our bigger-and-better society is now like a hypochondriac, so obsessed with its own economic health as to have lost the capacity to remain healthy. The whole world is so greedy for more bathtubs that it has lost the stability necessary to build them, or even to turn off the tap. Nothing could be more salutary at this stage than a little healthy contempt for a plethora of material blessings.

Perhaps such a shift of values can be achieved by reappraising things unnatural, tame, and confined in terms of things natural, wild, and free.

Aldo Leopold

Madison, Wisconsin, March 4, 1948

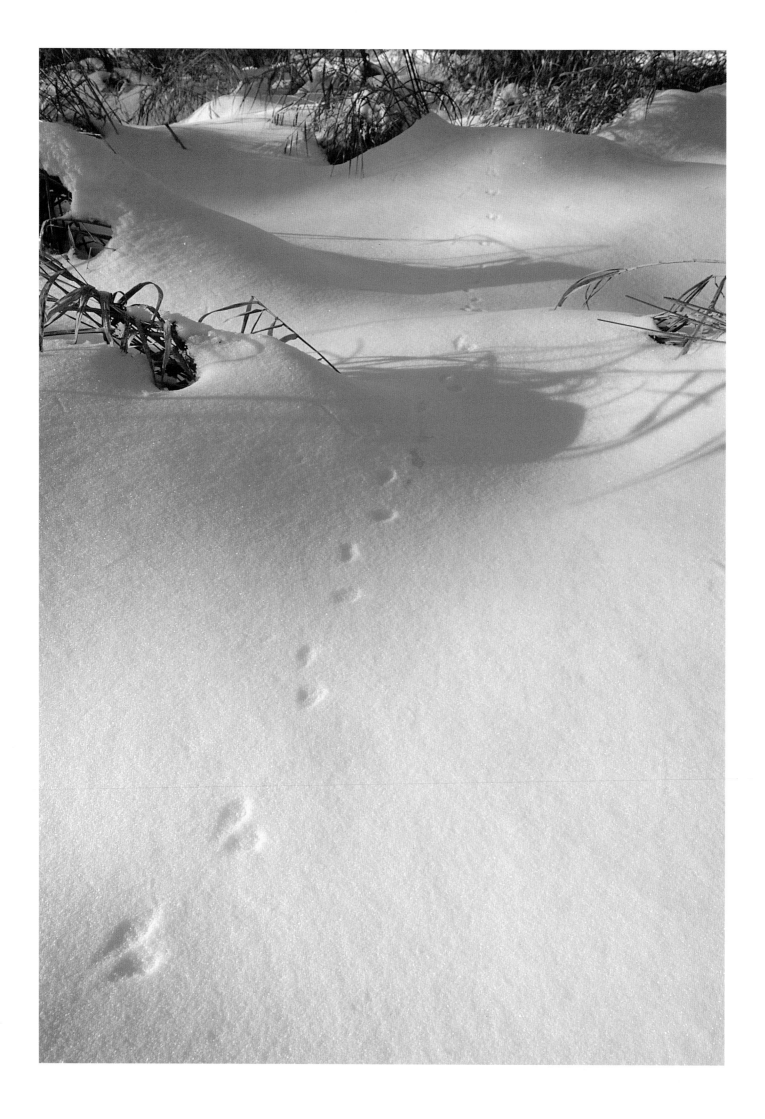

January

January Thaw

EACH YEAR, after the midwinter blizzards, there comes a night of thaw when the tinkle of dripping water is heard in the land. It brings strange stirrings, not only to creatures abed for the night, but to some who have been asleep for the winter. The hibernating skunk, curled up in his deep den, uncurls himself and ventures forth to prowl the wet world, dragging his belly in the snow. His track marks one of the earliest datable events in that cycle of beginnings and ceasings which we call a year.

The track is likely to display an indifference to mundane affairs uncommon at other seasons; it leads straight across-country, as if its maker had hitched his wagon to a star and dropped the reins. I follow, curious to deduce his state of mind and appetite, and destination if any.

❧   ❧   ❧

THE MONTHS OF THE YEAR, from January up to June, are a geometric progression in the abundance of distractions. In January one may follow a skunk track, or search for bands on the chickadees, or see what young pines the deer have browsed, or what muskrat houses the mink have dug, with only an occasional and mild digression into other doings. January observation can be almost as simple and peaceful as snow, and almost as continuous as cold. There is time not only to see who has done what, but to speculate why.

❧   ❧   ❧

A MEADOW MOUSE, startled by my approach, darts damply across the skunk track. Why is he abroad in daylight? Probably because he feels grieved about the thaw. Today his maze of secret tunnels, laboriously chewed through the matted grass under the snow, are tunnels no more, but only paths exposed to public view and ridicule. Indeed the thawing sun has mocked the basic premises of the microtine economic system!

The mouse is a sober citizen who knows that grass grows in order that mice may store it as underground haystacks, and that snow falls in order that mice may build subways from stack to stack: supply, demand, and transport all neatly organized. To the mouse, snow means freedom from want and fear.

Mouse tracks in snow

A ROUGH-LEGGED HAWK comes sailing over the meadow ahead. Now he stops, hovers like a kingfisher, and then drops like a feathered bomb into the marsh. He does not rise again, so I am sure he has caught, and is now eating, some worried mouse-engineer who could not wait until night to inspect the damage to his well-ordered world.

The rough-leg has no opinion why grass grows, but he is well aware that snow melts in order that hawks may again catch mice. He came down out of the Arctic in the hope of thaws, for to him a thaw means freedom from want and fear.

※　　　※　　　※

THE SKUNK TRACK ENTERS THE WOODS, and crosses a glade where the rabbits have packed down the snow with their tracks, and mottled it with pinkish urinations. Newly exposed oak seedlings have paid for the thaw with their newly barked stems. Tufts of rabbit-hair bespeak the year's first battles among the amorous bucks. Further on I find a bloody spot, encircled by a wide-sweeping arc of owl's wings. To this rabbit the thaw brought freedom from want, but also a reckless abandonment of fear. The owl has reminded him that thoughts of spring are no substitute for caution.

※　　　※　　　※

THE SKUNK TRACK LEADS ON, showing no interest in possible food, and no concern over the rompings or retributions of his neighbors. I wonder what he has on his mind; what got him out of bed? Can one impute romantic motives to this corpulent fellow, dragging his ample beltline through the slush? Finally the track enters a pile of drift-wood, and does not emerge. I hear the tinkle of dripping water among the logs, and I fancy the skunk hears it too. I turn homeward, still wondering.

The Great Marsh in winter

February

Good Oak

THERE ARE TWO SPIRITUAL DANGERS in not owning a farm. One is the danger of supposing that breakfast comes from the grocery, and the other that heat comes from the furnace.

To avoid the first danger, one should plant a garden, preferably where there is no grocer to confuse the issue.

To avoid the second, he should lay a split of good oak on the andirons, preferably where there is no furnace, and let it warm his shins while a February blizzard tosses the trees outside. If one has cut, split, hauled, and piled his own good oak, and let his mind work the while, he will remember much about where the heat comes from, and with a wealth of detail denied to those who spend the week end in town astride a radiator.

❧   ❧   ❧

THE PARTICULAR OAK NOW AGLOW on my andirons grew on the bank of the old emigrant road where it climbs the sandhill. The stump, which I measured upon felling the tree, has a diameter of 30 inches. It shows 80 growth rings, hence the seedling from which it originated must have laid its first ring of wood in 1865, at the end of the Civil War. But I know from the history of present seedlings that no oak grows above the reach of rabbits without a decade or more of getting girdled each winter, and re-sprouting during the following summer. Indeed, it is all too clear that every surviving oak is the product either of rabbit negligence or of rabbit scarcity. Some day some patient botanist will draw a frequency curve of oak birth-years, and show that the curve humps every ten years, each hump originating from a low in the ten-year rabbit cycle. (A fauna and flora, by this very process of perpetual battle within and among species, achieve collective immortality.)

Oak fire and Aldo's kettle, the Shack
Following pages: winter, sand counties

It is likely, then, that a low in rabbits occurred in the middle 'sixties, when my oak began to lay on annual rings, but that the acorn that produced it fell during the preceding decade, when the covered wagons were still passing over my road into the Great Northwest. It may have been the wash and wear of the emigrant traffic that bared this roadbank, and thus enabled this particular acorn to spread its first leaves to the sun. Only one acorn in a thousand ever grew large enough to fight rabbits; the rest were drowned at birth in the prairie sea.

It is a warming thought that this one wasn't, and thus lived to garner eighty years of June sun. It is this sunlight that is now being released, through the intervention of my axe and saw, to warm my shack and my spirit through eighty gusts of blizzard. And with each gust a wisp of smoke from my chimney bears witness, to whomsoever it may concern, that the sun did not shine in vain.

My dog does not care where heat comes from, but he cares ardently that it come, and soon. Indeed he considers my ability to make it come as something magical, for when I rise in the cold black pre-dawn and kneel shivering by the hearth making a fire, he pushes himself blandly between me and the kindling splits I have laid on the ashes, and I must touch a match to them by poking it between his legs. Such faith, I suppose, is the kind that moves mountains.

It was a bolt of lightning that put an end to wood-making by this particular oak. We were all awakened, one night in July, by the thunderous crash; we realized that the bolt must have hit near by, but, since it had not hit us, we all went back to sleep. Man brings all things to the test of himself, and this is notably true of lightning.

Next morning, as we strolled over the sandhill rejoicing with the cone-flowers and the prairie clovers over their fresh accession of rain, we came upon a great slab of bark freshly torn from the trunk of the roadside oak. The trunk showed a long spiral scar of barkless sapwood, a foot wide and not yet yellowed by the sun. By the next day the leaves had wilted, and we knew that the lightning had bequeathed to us three cords of prospective fuel wood.

We mourned the loss of the old tree, but knew that a dozen of its progeny standing straight and stalwart on the sands had already taken over its job of wood-making.

Cone-flowers in winter, Lissa's Prairie

We let the dead veteran season for a year in the sun it could no longer use, and then on a crisp winter's day we laid a newly filed saw to its bastioned base. Fragrant little chips of history spewed from the saw cut, and accumulated on the snow before each kneeling sawyer. We sensed that these two piles of sawdust were something more than wood: that they were the integrated transect of a century; that our saw was biting its way, stroke by stroke, decade by decade, into the chronology of a lifetime, written in concentric annual rings of good oak.

❧   ❧   ❧

IT TOOK ONLY A DOZEN PULLS OF THE SAW to transect the few years of our ownership, during which we had learned to love and cherish this farm. Abruptly we began to cut the years of our predecessor the bootlegger, who hated this farm, skinned it of residual fertility, burned its farmhouse, threw it back into the lap of the County (with delinquent taxes to boot), and then disappeared among the landless anonymities of the Great Depression. Yet the oak had laid down good wood for him; his sawdust was as fragrant, as sound, and as pink as our own. An oak is no respecter of persons.

The reign of the bootlegger ended sometime during the dust-bowl drouths of 1936, 1934, 1933, and 1930. Oak smoke from his still and peat from burning marshlands must have clouded the sun in those years, and alphabetical conservation was abroad in the land, but the sawdust shows no change.

Rest! cries the chief sawyer, and we pause for breath.

❧   ❧   ❧

NOW OUR SAW BITES INTO THE 1920'S, the Babbittian decade when everything grew bigger and better in heedlessness and arrogance—until 1929, when stock markets crumpled. If the oak heard them fall, its wood gives no sign. Nor did it heed the Legislature's several protestations of love for trees: a National Forest and a forest-crop law in 1927, a great refuge on the Upper Mississippi bottomlands in 1924, and a new forest policy in 1921. Neither did it notice the demise of the state's last marten in 1925, nor the arrival of its first starling in 1923.

In March 1922, the "Big Sleet" tore the neighboring elms limb from limb, but there is no sign of damage to our tree. What is a ton of ice, more or less, to a good oak?

Rest! cries the chief sawyer, and we pause for breath.

Oak with star trails

Now the saw bites into 1910-20, the decade of the drainage dream, when steam shovels sucked dry the marshes of central Wisconsin to make farms, and made ash-heaps instead. Our marsh escaped, not because of any caution or forbearance among engineers, but because the river floods it each April, and did so with a vengeance—perhaps a defensive vengeance—in the years 1913-16. The oak laid on wood just the same, even in 1915, when the Supreme Court abolished the state forests and Governor Phillip pontificated that "state forestry is not a good business proposition." (It did not occur to the Governor that there might be more than one definition of what is good, and even of what is business. It did not occur to him that while the courts were writing one definition of goodness in the law books, fires were writing quite another one on the face of the land. Perhaps, to be a governor, one must be free from doubt on such matters.)

While forestry receded during this decade, game conservation advanced. In 1916 pheasants became successfully established in Waukesha County; in 1915 a federal law prohibited spring shooting; in 1913 a state game farm was started; in 1912 a "buck law" protected female deer; in 1911 an epidemic of refuges spread over the state. "Refuge" became a holy word, but the oak took no heed.

Rest! cries the chief sawyer, and we pause for breath.

❧　　　❧　　　❧

Now we cut 1910, when a great university president published a book on conservation, a great sawfly epidemic killed millions of tamaracks, a great drouth burned the pineries, and a great dredge drained Horicon Marsh.

We cut 1909, when smelt were first planted in the Great Lakes, and when a wet summer induced the Legislature to cut the forest-fire appropriations.

We cut 1908, a dry year when the forests burned fiercely, and Wisconsin parted with its last cougar.

We cut 1907, when a wandering lynx, looking in the wrong direction for the promised land, ended his career among the farms of Dane County.

We cut 1906, when the first state forester took office, and fires burned 17,000 acres in these sand counties; we cut 1905 when a great flight of goshawks came out of the North and ate up the local grouse (they no doubt perched in this tree to eat some of mine). We cut 1902-3, a winter of bitter cold; 1901, which brought the most intense drouth of record (rainfall only 17 inches); 1900, a centennial year of hope, of prayer, and the usual annual ring of oak.

Rest! cries the chief sawyer, and we pause for breath.

NOW OUR SAW BITES INTO THE 1890'S, called gay by those whose eyes turn cityward rather than landward. We cut 1899, when the last passenger pigeon collided with a charge of shot near Babcock, two counties to the north; we cut 1898 when a dry fall, followed by a snowless winter, froze the soil seven feet deep and killed the apple trees; 1897, another drouth year, when another forestry commission came into being; 1896, when 25,000 prairie chickens were shipped to market from the village of Spooner alone; 1895, another year of fires; 1894, another drouth year; and 1893, the year of "The Bluebird Storm," when a March blizzard reduced the migrating bluebirds to near-zero. (The first bluebirds always alighted in this oak, but in the middle 'nineties it must have gone without.) We cut 1892, another year of fires; 1891, a low in the grouse cycle; and 1890, the year of the Babcock Milk Tester, which enabled Governor Heil to boast, half a century later, that Wisconsin is America's Dairyland. The motor licenses which now parade that boast were then not foreseen, even by Professor Babcock.

It was likewise in 1890 that the largest pine rafts in history slipped down the Wisconsin River in full view of my oak, to build an empire of red barns for the cows of the prairie states. Thus it is that good pine now stands between the cow and the blizzard, just as good oak stands between the blizzard and me.

Rest! cries the chief sawyer, and we pause for breath.

❧   ❧   ❧

NOW OUR SAW BITES INTO THE 1880'S; into 1889, a drouth year in which Arbor Day was first proclaimed; into 1887, when Wisconsin appointed its first game wardens; into 1886, when the College of Agriculture held its first short course for farmers; into 1885, preceded by a winter "of unprecedented length and severity"; into 1883, when Dean W. H. Henry reported that the spring flowers at Madison bloomed 13 days later than average; into 1882, the year Lake Mendota opened a month late following the historic "Big Snow" and bitter cold of 1881-2.

It was likewise in 1881 that the Wisconsin Agricultural Society debated the question, "How do you account for the second growth of black oak timber that has sprung up all over the country in the last thirty years?" My oak was one of these. One debater claimed spontaneous generation, another claimed regurgitation of acorns by southbound pigeons.

Rest! cries the chief sawyer, and we pause for breath.

NOW OUR SAW BITES THE 1870'S, the decade of Wisconsin's carousal in wheat. Monday morning came in 1879, when chinch bugs, grubs, rust, and soil exhaustion finally convinced Wisconsin farmers that they could not compete with the virgin prairies further west in the game of wheating land to death. I suspect that this farm played its share in the game, and that the sand blow just north of my oak had its origin in over-wheating.

This same year of 1879 saw the first planting of carp in Wisconsin, and also the first arrival of quack-grass as a stowaway from Europe. On 27 October 1879, six migrating prairie chickens perched on the rooftree of the German Methodist Church in Madison, and took a look at the growing city. On 8 November the markets at Madison were reported to be glutted with ducks at 10 cents each.

In 1878 a deer hunter from Sauk Rapids remarked prophetically, "The hunters promise to outnumber the deer."

On 10 September 1877, two brothers, shooting Muskego Lake, bagged 210 blue-winged teal in one day.

In 1876 came the wettest year of record; the rainfall piled up 50 inches. Prairie chickens declined, perhaps owing to hard rains.

In 1875 four hunters killed 153 prairie chickens at York Prairie, one county to the eastward. In the same year the U.S. Fish Commission planted Atlantic salmon in Devil's Lake, 10 miles south of my oak.

In 1874 the first factory-made barbed wire was stapled to oak trees; I hope no such artifacts are buried in the oak now under saw!

In 1873 one Chicago firm received and marketed 25,000 prairie chickens. The Chicago trade collectively bought 600,000 at $3.25 per dozen.

Prairie chickens

In 1872 the last wild Wisconsin turkey was killed, two counties to the southwest.

It is appropriate that the decade ending the pioneer carousal in wheat should likewise have ended the pioneer carousal in pigeon blood. In 1871, within a 50-mile triangle spreading northwestward from my oak, 136 million pigeons are estimated to have nested, and some may have nested in it, for it was then a thrifty sapling 20 feet tall. Pigeon hunters by scores plied their trade with net and gun, club and salt lick, and trainloads of prospective pigeon pie moved southward and eastward toward the cities. It was the last big nesting in Wisconsin, and nearly the last in any state.

This same year 1871 brought other evidence of the march of empire: the Peshtigo Fire, which cleared a couple of counties of trees and soil, and the Chicago Fire, said to have started from the protesting kick of a cow.

In 1870 the meadow mice had already staged their march of empire; they ate up the young orchards of the young state, and then died. They did not eat my oak, whose bark was already too tough and thick for mice.

It was likewise in 1870 that a market gunner boasted in the *American Sportsman* of killing 6000 ducks in one season near Chicago.

Rest! cries the chief sawyer, and we pause for breath.

93   93   93

OUR SAW NOW CUTS THE 1860'S, when thousands died to settle the question: Is the man-man community lightly to be dismembered? They settled it, but they did not see, nor do we yet see, that the same question applies to the man-land community.

This decade was not without its gropings toward the larger issue. In 1867 Increase A. Lapham induced the State Horticultural Society to offer prizes for forest plantations. In 1866 the last native Wisconsin elk was killed. The saw now severs 1865, the pith-year of our oak. In that year John Muir offered to buy from his brother, who then owned the home farm thirty miles east of my oak, a sanctuary for the wildflowers that had gladdened his youth. His brother declined to part with the land, but he could not suppress the idea: 1865 still stands in Wisconsin history as the birthyear of mercy for things natural, wild, and free.

We have cut the core. Our saw now reverses its orientation in history; we cut backward across the years, and outward toward the far side of the stump. At last there is a tremor in the great trunk; the saw-kerf suddenly widens; the saw is quickly pulled as the sawyers spring backward to safety; all hands cry "Timber!"; my oak leans, groans, and crashes with earth-shaking thunder, to lie prostrate across the emigrant road that gave it birth.

❅   ❅   ❅

NOW COMES THE JOB of making wood. The maul rings on steel wedges as the sections of trunk are up-ended one by one, only to fall apart in fragrant slabs to be corded by the roadside.

There is an allegory for historians in the diverse functions of saw, wedge, and axe.

The saw works only across the years, which it must deal with one by one, in sequence. From each year the raker teeth pull little chips of fact, which accumulate in little piles, called sawdust by woodsmen and archives by historians; both judge the character of what lies within by the character of the samples thus made visible without. It is not until the transect is completed that the tree falls, and the stump yields a collective view of a century. By its fall the tree attests the unity of the hodge-podge called history.

The wedge, on the other hand, works only in radial splits; such a split yields a collective view of all the years at once, or no view at all, depending on the skill with which the plane of the split is chosen. (If in doubt, let the section season for a year until a crack develops. Many a hastily driven wedge lies rusting in the woods, embedded in unsplittable cross-grain.)

The axe functions only at an angle diagonal to the years, and this only for the peripheral rings of the recent past. Its special function is to lop limbs, for which both saw and wedge are useless.

The three tools are requisite to good oak, and to good history.

❅   ❅   ❅

THESE THINGS I PONDER AS THE KETTLE SINGS, and the good oak burns to red coals on white ashes. Those ashes, come spring, I will return to the orchard at the foot of the sandhill. They will come back to me again, perhaps as red apples, or perhaps as a spirit of enterprise in some fat October squirrel, who, for reasons unknown to himself, is bent on planting acorns.

March

The Geese Return

ONE SWALLOW DOES NOT MAKE A SUMMER, but one skein of geese, cleaving the murk of a March thaw, is the spring.

A cardinal, whistling spring to a thaw but later finding himself mistaken, can retrieve his error by resuming his winter silence. A chipmunk, emerging for a sunbath but finding a blizzard, has only to go back to bed. But a migrating goose, staking two hundred miles of black night on the chance of finding a hole in the lake, has no easy chance for retreat. His arrival carries the conviction of a prophet who has burned his bridges.

Canada geese landing on Singer Pond

A March morning is only as drab as he who walks in it without a glance skyward, ear cocked for geese. I once knew an educated lady, banded by Phi Beta Kappa, who told me that she had never heard or seen the geese that twice a year proclaim the revolving seasons to her well-insulated roof. Is education possibly a process of trading awareness for things of lesser worth? The goose who trades his is soon a pile of feathers.

The geese that proclaim the seasons to our farm are aware of many things, including the Wisconsin statutes. The southbound November flocks pass over us high and haughty, with scarcely a honk of recognition for their favorite sandbars and sloughs. "As a crow flies" is crooked compared with their undeviating aim at the nearest big lake twenty miles to the south, where they loaf by day on broad waters and filch corn by night from the freshly cut stubbles. November geese are aware that every marsh and pond bristles from dawn till dark with hopeful guns.

March geese are a different story. Although they have been shot at most of the winter, as attested by their buckshot-battered pinions, they know that the spring truce is now in effect. They wind the oxbows of the river, cutting low over the now gunless points and islands, and gabbling to each sandbar as to a long-lost friend. They weave low over the marshes and meadows, greeting each newly melted puddle and pool. Finally, after a few *pro-forma* circlings of our marsh, they set wing and glide silently to the pond, black landing-gear lowered and rumps white against the far hill. Once touching water, our newly arrived guests set up a honking and splashing that shakes the last thought of winter out of the brittle cattails. Our geese are home again!

It is at this moment of each year that I wish I were a muskrat, eye-deep in the marsh.

Muskrat at sunset

Once the first geese are in, they honk a clamorous invitation to each migrating flock, and in a few days the marsh is full of them. On our farm we measure the amplitude of our spring by two yardsticks: the number of pines planted, and the number of geese that stop. Our record is 642 geese counted in on 11 April 1946.

As in fall, our spring geese make daily trips to corn, but these are no surreptitious sneakings-out by night; the flocks move noisily to and from corn stubbles through the day. Each departure is preceded by loud gustatory debate, and each return by an even louder one. The returning flocks, once thoroughly at home, omit their *pro-forma* circlings of the marsh. They tumble out of the sky like maple leaves, side-slipping right and left to lose altitude, feet spraddled toward the shouts of welcome below. I suppose the ensuing gabble deals with the merits of the day's dinner. They are now eating the waste corn that the snow blanket has protected over winter from corn-seeking crows, cottontails, meadow mice, and pheasants.

It is a conspicuous fact that the corn stubbles selected by geese for feeding are usually those occupying former prairies. No man knows whether this bias for prairie corn reflects some superior nutritional value, or some ancestral tradition transmitted from generation to generation since the prairie days. Perhaps it reflects the simpler fact that prairie cornfields tend to be large. If I could understand the thunderous debates that precede and follow these daily excursions to corn, I might soon learn the reason for the prairie-bias. But I cannot, and I am well content that it should remain a mystery. What a dull world if we knew all about geese!

Canada geese, the Great Marsh

In thus watching the daily routine of a spring goose convention, one notices the prevalence of singles—lone geese that do much flying about and much talking. One is apt to impute a disconsolate tone to their honkings, and to jump to the conclusion that they are broken-hearted widowers, or mothers hunting lost children. The seasoned ornithologist knows, however, that such subjective interpretation of bird behavior is risky. I long tried to keep an open mind on the question.

After my students and I had counted for half a dozen years the number of geese comprising a flock, some unexpected light was cast on the meaning of lone geese. It was found by mathematical analysis that flocks of six or multiples of six were far more frequent than chance alone would dictate. In other words, goose flocks are families, or aggregations of families, and lone geese in spring are probably just what our fond imaginings had first suggested. They are bereaved survivors of the winter's shooting, searching in vain for their kin. Now I am free to grieve with and for the lone honkers.

It is not often that cold-potato mathematics thus confirms the sentimental promptings of the bird-lover.

Six geese at sunrise

On April nights when it has become warm enough to sit outdoors, we love to listen to the proceedings of the convention in the marsh. There are long periods of silence when one hears only the winnowing of snipe, the hoot of a distant owl, or the nasal clucking of some amorous coot. Then, of a sudden, a strident honk resounds, and in an instant pandemonium echoes. There is a beating of pinions on water, a rushing of dark prows propelled by churning paddles, and a general shouting by the onlookers of a vehement controversy. Finally some deep honker has his last word, and the noise subsides to that half-audible small-talk that seldom ceases among geese. Once again, I would I were a muskrat!

By the time the pasques are in full bloom our goose convention dwindles, and before May our marsh is once again a mere grassy wetness, enlivened only by redwings and rails.

❧ ❧ ❧

IT IS AN IRONY OF HISTORY that the great powers should have discovered the unity of nations at Cairo in 1943. The geese of the world have had that notion for a longer time, and each March they stake their lives on its essential truth.

In the beginning there was only the unity of the Ice Sheet. Then followed the unity of the March thaw, and the northward hegira of the international geese. Every March since the Pleistocene, the geese have honked unity from China Sea to Siberian Steppe, from Euphrates to Volga, from Nile to Murmansk, from Lincolnshire to Spitsbergen. Every March since the Pleistocene, the geese have honked unity from Currituck to Labrador, Matamuskeet to Ungava, Horseshoe Lake to Hudson's Bay, Avery Island to Baffin Land, Panhandle to Mackenzie, Sacramento to Yukon.

By this international commerce of geese, the waste corn of Illinois is carried through the clouds to the Arctic tundras, there to combine with the waste sunlight of a nightless June to grow goslings for all the lands between. And in this annual barter of food for light, and winter warmth for summer solitude, the whole continent receives as net profit a wild poem dropped from the murky skies upon the muds of March.

Dusk, the Great Marsh

Following pages: migrating geese

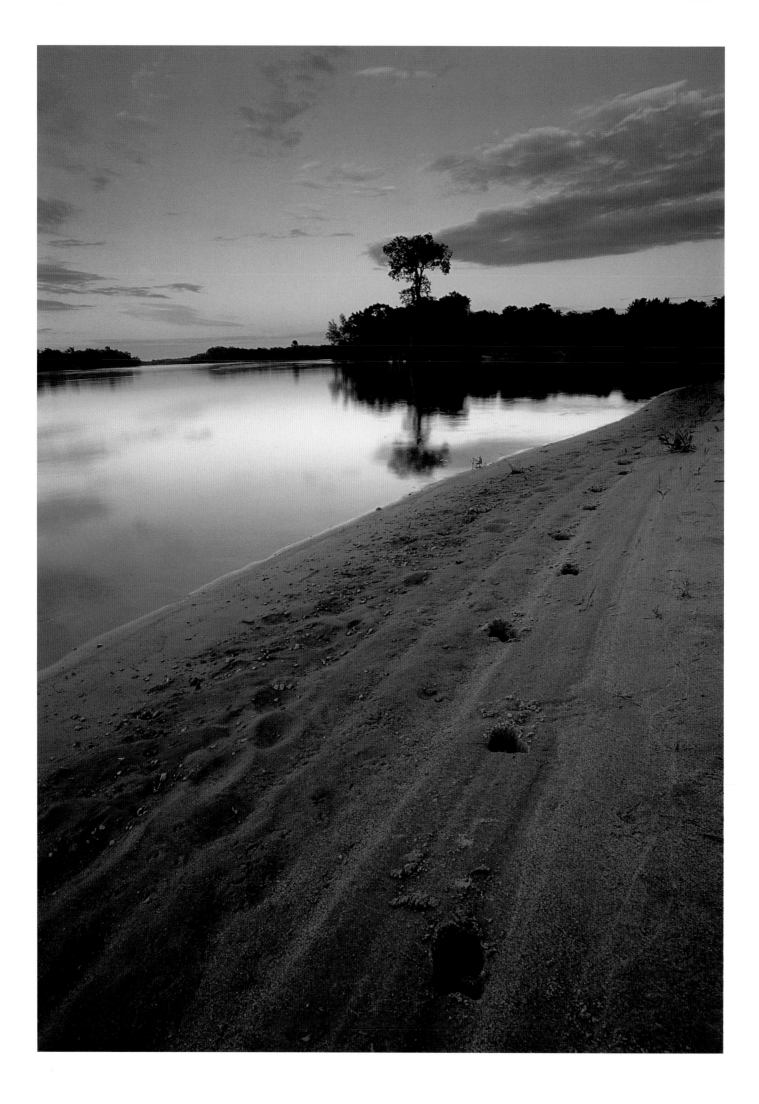

April

Come High Water

THE SAME LOGIC THAT CAUSES BIG RIVERS ALWAYS TO FLOW past big cities causes cheap farms sometimes to be marooned by spring floods. Ours is a cheap farm, and sometimes when we visit it in April we get marooned.

Not intentionally, of course, but one can, to a degree, guess from weather reports when the snows up north will melt, and one can estimate how many days it takes for the flood to run the gauntlet of upriver cities. Thus, come Sunday evening, one must go back to town and work, but one can't. How sweetly the spreading waters murmur condolence for the wreckage they have inflicted on Monday morning dates! How deep and chesty the honkings of the geese as they cruise over cornfield after cornfield, each in process of becoming a lake. Every hundred yards some new goose flails the air as he struggles to lead the echelon in its morning survey of this new and watery world.

The enthusiasm of geese for high water is a subtle thing, and might be overlooked by those unfamiliar with goose-gossip, but the enthusiasm of carp is obvious and unmistakable. No sooner has the rising flood wetted the grass roots than here they come, rooting and wallowing with the prodigious zest of pigs turned out to pasture, flashing red tails and yellow bellies, cruising the wagon tracks and cow-paths, and shaking the reeds and bushes in their haste to explore what to them is an expanding universe.

Unlike the geese and the carp, the terrestrial birds and mammals accept high water with philosophical detachment. A cardinal atop a river birch whistles loudly his claim to a territory that, but for the trees, cannot be seen to exist. A ruffed grouse drums from the flooded woods; he must be perched on the high end of his highest drumming log. Meadow-mice paddle ridgeward with the calm assurance of miniature muskrats. From the orchard bounds a deer, evicted from his usual daytime bed in the willow thickets. Everywhere are rabbits, calmly accepting quarters on our hill, which serves, in Noah's absence, for an ark.

Deer tracks on the Leopolds' beach, Wisconsin River

The spring flood brings us more than high adventure; it brings likewise an unpredictable miscellany of floatable objects pilfered from upriver farms. An old board stranded on our meadow has, to us, twice the value of the same piece new from the lumberyard. Each old board has its own individual history, always unknown, but always to some degree guessable from the kind of wood, its dimensions, its nails, screws, or paint, its finish or the lack of it, its wear or decay. One can even guess, from the abrasion of its edges and ends on sandbars, how many floods have carried it in years past.

Our lumber pile, recruited entirely from the river, is thus not only a collection of personalities, but an anthology of human strivings in upriver farms and forests. The autobiography of an old board is a kind of literature not yet taught on campuses, but any riverbank farm is a library where he who hammers or saws may read at will. Come high water, there is always an accession of new books.

※   ※   ※

THERE ARE DEGREES AND KINDS of solitude. An island in a lake has one kind; but lakes have boats, and there is always the chance that one might land to pay you a visit. A peak in the clouds has another kind; but most peaks have trails, and trails have tourists. I know of no solitude so secure as one guarded by a spring flood; nor do the geese, who have seen more kinds and degrees of aloneness than I have.

So we sit on our hill beside a new-blown pasque, and watch the geese go by. I see our road dipping gently into the waters, and I conclude (with inner glee but exterior detachment) that the question of traffic, in or out, is for this day at least, debatable only among carp.

Weathered wood, the Shack

Draba

WITHIN A FEW WEEKS NOW DRABA, the smallest flower that blows, will sprinkle every sandy place with small blooms.

He who hopes for spring with upturned eye never sees so small a thing as Draba. He who despairs of spring with downcast eye steps on it, unknowing. He who searches for spring with his knees in the mud finds it, in abundance.

Draba asks, and gets, but scant allowance of warmth and comfort; it subsists on the leavings of unwanted time and space. Botany books give it two or three lines, but never a plate or portrait. Sand too poor and sun too weak for bigger, better blooms are good enough for Draba. After all it is no spring flower, but only a postscript to a hope.

Draba plucks no heartstrings. Its perfume, if there is any, is lost in the gusty winds. Its color is plain white. Its leaves wear a sensible woolly coat. Nothing eats it; it is too small. No poets sing of it. Some botanist once gave it a Latin name, and then forgot it. Altogether it is of no importance—just a small creature that does a small job quickly and well.

Draba in late spring

Bur Oak

WHEN SCHOOL CHILDREN VOTE ON A STATE BIRD, flower, or tree, they are not making a decision; they are merely ratifying history. Thus history made bur oak the characteristic tree of southern Wisconsin when the prairie grasses first gained possession of the region. Bur oak is the only tree that can stand up to a prairie fire and live.

Have you ever wondered why a thick crust of corky bark covers the whole tree, even to the smallest twigs? This cork is armor. Bur oaks were the shock troops sent by the invading forest to storm the prairie; fire is what they had to fight. Each April, before the new grasses had covered the prairie with unburnable greenery, fires ran at will over the land, sparing only such old oaks as had grown bark too thick to scorch. Most of these groves of scattered veterans, known to the pioneers as "oak openings," consisted of bur oaks.

Engineers did not discover insulation; they copied it from these old soldiers of the prairie war. Botanists can read the story of that war for twenty thousand years. The record consists partly of pollen grains embedded in peats, partly of relic plants interned in the rear of the battle, and there forgotten. The record shows that the forest front at times retreated almost to Lake Superior; at times it advanced far to the south. At one period it advanced so far southward that spruce and other "rear guard" species grew to and beyond the southern border of Wisconsin; spruce pollen appears at a certain level in all peat bogs of the region. But the average battle line between prairie and forest was about where it is now, and the net outcome of the battle was a draw.

Bur oak with bark burn

One reason for this was that there were allies that threw their support first to one side, then to the other. Thus rabbits and mice mowed down the prairie herbs in summer, and in winter girdled any oak seedlings that survived the fires. Squirrels planted acorns in fall, and ate them all the rest of the year. June beetles undermined the prairie sod in their grub stage, but defoliated the oaks in their adult stage. But for this geeing and hawing of allies, and hence of the victory, we should not have today that rich mosaic of prairie and forest soils which looks so decorative on a map.

Jonathan Carver has left us a vivid word-picture of the prairie border in pre-settlement days. On 10 October 1763, he visited Blue Mounds, a group of high hills (now wooded) near the southwestern corner of Dane County. He says:

> I ascended one of the highest of these, and had an extensive view of the country. For many miles nothing was to be seen but lesser mountains, which appeared at a distance like haycocks, they being free from trees. Only a few groves of hickory, and stunted oaks, covered some of the vallies.

In the 1840's a new animal, the settler, intervened in the prairie battle. He didn't mean to, he just plowed enough fields to deprive the prairie of its immemorial ally: fire. Seedling oaks forthwith romped over the grasslands in legions, and what had been the prairie region became a region of woodlot farms. If you doubt this story, go count the rings on any set of stumps on any "ridge" woodlot in southwest Wisconsin. All the trees except the oldest veterans date back to the 1850's and the 1860's, and this was when fires ceased on the prairie.

John Muir grew up in Marquette County during this period when new woods overrode the old prairies and engulfed the oak openings in thickets of saplings. In his *Boyhood and Youth* he recalls that:

> The uniformly rich soil of the Illinois and Wisconsin prairies produced so close and tall a growth of grasses for fires that no tree could live on it. Had there been no fires, these fine prairies, so marked a feature of the country, would have been covered by the heaviest forest. As soon as the oak openings were settled, and the farmers had prevented running grass-fires, the grubs [roots] grew up into trees and formed tall thickets so dense that it was difficult to walk through them, and every trace of the sunny [oak] "openings" vanished.

Thus, he who owns a veteran bur oak owns more than a tree. He owns a historical library, and a reserved seat in the theater of evolution. To the discerning eye, his farm is labeled with the badge and symbol of the prairie war.

Red squirrel

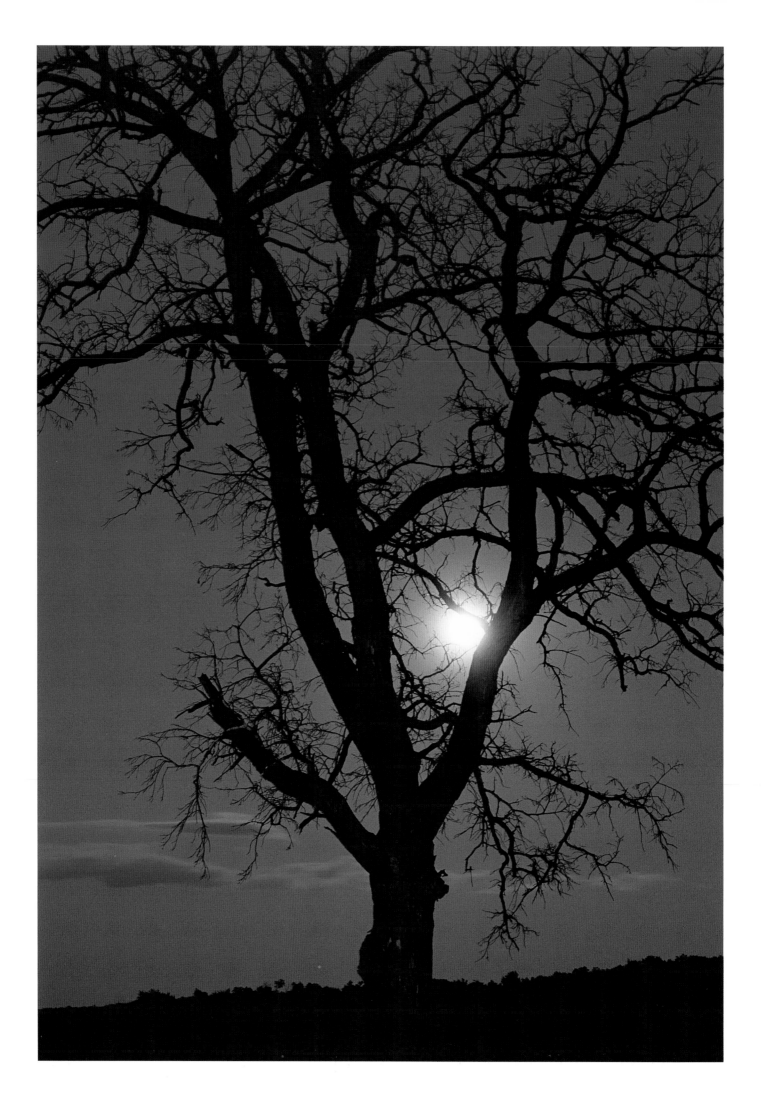

Sky Dance

I OWNED MY FARM FOR TWO YEARS before learning that the sky dance is to be seen over my woods every evening in April and May. Since we discovered it, my family and I have been reluctant to miss even a single performance.

The show begins on the first warm evening in April at exactly 6:50 p.m. The curtain goes up one minute later each day until 1 June, when the time is 7:50. This sliding scale is dictated by vanity, the dancer demanding a romantic light intensity of exactly 0.05 foot-candles. Do not be late, and sit quietly, lest he fly away in a huff.

The stage props, like the opening hour, reflect the temperamental demands of the performer. The stage must be an open amphitheater in woods or brush, and in its center there must be a mossy spot, a streak of sterile sand, a bare outcrop of rock, or a bare roadway. Why the male woodcock should be such a stickler for a bare dance floor puzzled me at first, but I now think it is a matter of legs. The woodcock's legs are short, and his struttings cannot be executed to advantage in dense grass or weeds, nor could his lady see them there. I have more woodcocks than most farmers because I have more mossy sand, too poor to support grass.

Knowing the place and the hour, you seat yourself under a bush to the east of the dance floor and wait, watching against the sunset for the woodcock's arrival. He flies in low from some neighboring thicket, alights on the bare moss, and at once begins the overture: a series of queer throaty *peents* spaced about two seconds apart, and sounding much like the summer call of the nighthawk.

Suddenly the peenting ceases and the bird flutters skyward in a series of wide spirals, emitting a musical twitter. Up and up he goes, the spirals steeper and smaller, the twittering louder and louder, until the performer is only a speck in the sky. Then, without warning, he tumbles like a crippled plane, giving voice in a soft liquid warble that a March bluebird might envy. At a few feet from the ground he levels off and returns to his peenting ground, usually to the exact spot where the performance began, and there resumes his peenting.

It is soon too dark to see the bird on the ground, but you can see his flights against the sky for an hour, which is the usual duration of the show. On moonlight nights, however, it may continue, at intervals, as long as the moon continues to shine.

Full moon and oak, the farm

At daybreak the whole show is repeated. In early April the final curtain falls at 5:15 a.m.; the time advances two minutes a day until June, when the performance closes for the year at 3:15. Why the disparity in sliding scale? Alas, I fear that even romance tires, for it takes only a fifth as much light to stop the sky dance at dawn as suffices to start it at sunset.

❦   ❦   ❦

IT IS FORTUNATE, perhaps, that no matter how intently one studies the hundred little dramas of the woods and meadows, one can never learn all of the salient facts about any one of them. What I do not yet know about the sky dance is: where is the lady, and just what part, if any, does she play? I often see two woodcocks on a peenting ground, and the two sometimes fly together, but they never peent together. Is the second bird the hen, or a rival male?

Another unknown: is the twitter vocal, or is it mechanical? My friend, Bill Feeney, once clapped a net over a peenting bird and removed his outer primary wing feathers; thereafter the bird peented and warbled, but twittered no more. But one such experiment is hardly conclusive.

Another unknown: up to what stage of nesting does the male continue the sky dance? My daughter once saw a bird peenting within twenty yards of a nest containing hatched shells, but was this *his* lady's nest? Or is this secretive fellow possibly bigamous without our ever having found it out? These, and many other questions, remain mysteries of the deepening dusk.

The drama of the sky dance is enacted nightly on hundreds of farms, the owners of which sigh for entertainment, but harbor the illusion that it is to be sought in theaters. They live on the land, but not by the land.

The woodcock is a living refutation of the theory that the utility of a game bird is to serve as a target, or to pose gracefully on a slice of toast. No one would rather hunt woodcock in October than I, but since learning of the sky dance I find myself calling one or two birds enough. I must be sure that, come April, there be no dearth of dancers in the sunset sky.

Woodcock feathers

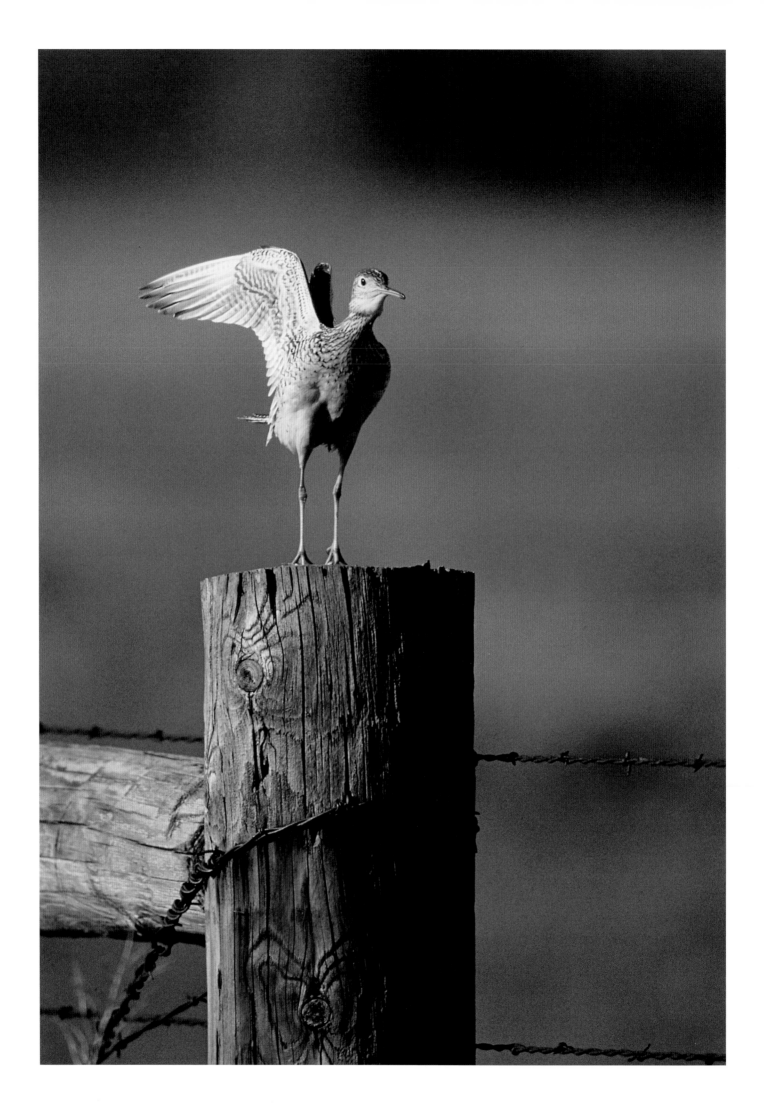

May

Back from the Argentine

WHEN DANDELIONS HAVE SET THE MARK OF MAY ON WISCONSIN PASTURES, it is time to listen for the final proof of spring. Sit down on a tussock, cock your ears at the sky, dial out the bedlam of meadowlarks and redwings, and soon you may hear it: the flight-song of the upland plover, just now back from the Argentine.

If your eyes are strong, you may search the sky and see him, wings aquiver, circling among the woolly clouds. If your eyes are weak, don't try it; just watch the fence posts. Soon a flash of silver will tell you on which post the plover has alighted and folded his long wings. Whoever invented the word "grace" must have seen the wing-folding of the plover.

There he sits; his whole being says it's your next move to absent yourself from his domain. The county records may allege that you own this pasture, but the plover airily rules out such trivial legalities. He has just flown 4000 miles to reassert the title he got from the Indians, and until the young plovers are a-wing, this pasture is his, and none may trespass without his protest.

Somewhere near by, the hen plover is brooding the four large pointed eggs which will shortly hatch four precocial chicks. From the moment their down is dry, they scamper through the grass like mice on stilts, quite able to elude your clumsy efforts to catch them. At thirty days the chicks are full grown; no other fowl develops with equal speed. By August they have graduated from flying school, and on cool August nights you can hear their whistled signals as they set wing for the pampas, to prove again the age-old unity of the Americas. Hemisphere solidarity is new among statesmen, but not among the feathered navies of the sky.

Upland plover folding wings

The upland plover fits easily into the agricultural countryside. He follows the black-and-white buffalo, which now pasture his prairies, and finds them an acceptable substitute for brown ones. He nests in hayfields as well as pastures, but, unlike the clumsy pheasant, does not get caught in hay mowers. Well before the hay is ready to cut, the young plovers are a-wing and away. In farm country, the plover has only two real enemies: the gully and the drainage ditch. Perhaps we shall one day find that these are our enemies, too.

There was a time in the early 1900's when Wisconsin farms nearly lost their immemorial timepiece, when May pastures greened in silence, and August nights brought no whistled reminder of impending fall. Universal gunpowder, plus the lure of plover-on-toast for post-Victorian banquets, had taken too great a toll. The belated protection of the federal migratory bird laws came just in time.

Wildflowers, Charlie's Prairie

June

The Alder Fork—*A Fishing Idyl*

WE FOUND THE MAIN STREAM SO LOW that the teeter-snipe pattered about in what last year were trout riffles, and so warm that we could duck in its deepest pool without a shout. Even after our cooling swim, waders felt like hot tar paper in the sun.

The evening's fishing proved as disappointing as its auguries. We asked that stream for trout, and it gave us a chub. That night we sat under a mosquito smudge and debated the morrow's plan. Two hundred miles of hot, dusty road we had come, to feel again the impetuous tug of a disillusioned brook or rainbow. There were no trout.

But this, we now remembered, was a stream of parts. High up near the headwaters we had once seen a fork, narrow, deep, and fed by cold springs that gurgled out under its close-hemmed walls of alder. What would a self-respecting trout do in such weather? Just what we did: go up.

In the fresh of the morning, when a hundred whitethroats had forgotten it would ever again be anything but sweet and cool, I climbed down the dewy bank and stepped into the Alder Fork. A trout was rising just upstream. I paid out some line—wishing it would always stay thus soft and dry—and, measuring the distance with a false cast or two, laid down a spent gnat exactly a foot above his last swirl. Forgotten now were the hot miles, the mosquitoes, the ignominious chub. He took it with one great gulp, and shortly I could hear him kicking in the bed of wet alder leaves at the bottom of the creel.

Another, albeit larger, fish had meanwhile risen in the next pool, which lay at the very "head of navigation," for at its upper end the alders closed in solid phalanx. One bush, with its brown stem laved in the middle current, shook with a perpetual silent laughter, as if to mock at any fly that gods or men might cast one inch beyond its outermost leaf.

Aldo's rod and grandson's reel

For the duration of a cigarette I sit on a rock midstream—and watch my trout rise under his guardian bush, while my rod and line hang drying on the alders of the sunny bank. Then—for prudence' sake—a little longer. That pool is too smooth up there. A breeze is stirring and may shortly ruffle it for an instant, and thus make more deadly that perfect cast I shall shortly lay upon its bosom.

It will come—a puff strong enough to shake a brown miller off the laughing alder, and cast it upon the pool.

Ready now! Coil up the dry line and stand midstream, rod in instant readiness. It's coming—a little premonitory shiver in that aspen on the hill lets me get out half a cast, and swish it gently back and forth, ready for the main puff to hit the pool. No more than half a line, mind you! The sun is high now, and any flicking shadow overhead would forewarn my hunker of his impending fate. Now! The last three yards shoot out, the fly falls gracefully at the feet of the laughing alder—he has it! I set hard to hold him out of the jungle beyond. He rushes downstream. In a few minutes he, too, is kicking in the creel.

I sit in happy meditation on my rock, pondering, while my line dries again, upon the ways of trout and men. How like fish we are: ready, nay eager, to seize upon whatever new thing some wind of circumstance shakes down upon the river of time! And how we rue our haste, finding the gilded morsel to contain a hook. Even so, I think there is some virtue in eagerness, whether its object prove true or false. How utterly dull would be a wholly prudent man, or trout, or world! Did I say a while ago that I waited "for prudence' sake"? That was not so. The only prudence in fishermen is that designed to set the stage for taking yet another, and perhaps a longer, chance.

Time to be at it now—they will soon stop rising. I wade waist deep to head of navigation, poke my head insolently into the shaking alder, and look within. Jungle is right! A coal-black hole above, so canopied in greenness you could not wave a fern, much less a rod, above its rushing depths. And there, almost rubbing his ribs against the dark bank, a great trout rolls lazily over as he sucks down a passing bug.

Not a chance to stalk him, even with the lowly worm. But twenty yards above I see bright sunshine on the water—another opening. Fish a dry fly downstream? It cannot, but it must, be done.

Brook trout detail

I retreat and climb the bank. Neck deep in jewel-weed and nettles, I detour through the alder thicket to the opening above. With cat-like care not to roil his majesty's bath, I step in, and stand stock-still for five minutes to let things calm down. The while, I strip out, oil, dry, and coil upon my left hand thirty feet of line. I am that far above the portal to the jungle.

Now for the long chance! I blow upon my fly to give it one last fluff, lay it on the stream at my feet, and quickly pay out coil after coil. Then, just as the line straightens out and the fly is sucked into the jungle, I walk quickly downstream, straining my eyes into the dark vault to follow its fortunes. A fleeting glimpse or two as it passes a speck of sunlight shows it still rides clear. It rounds the bend. In no time—long before the roil of my walking has betrayed the ruse—it reaches the black pool. I hear, rather than see, the rush of the great fish; I set hard, and the battle is on.

No prudent man would risk a dollar's worth of fly and leader pulling a trout upstream through the giant toothbrush of alder stems comprising the bend of that creek. But, as I said, no prudent man is a fisherman. By and by, with much cautious unraveling, I got him up into open water, and finally aboard the creel.

I shall now confess to you that none of those three trout had to be beheaded, or folded double, to fit their casket. What was big was not the trout, but the chance. What was full was not my creel, but my memory. Like the white-throats, I had forgotten it would ever again be aught but morning on the Fork.

Black water, Alder Creek

July

Great Possessions

ONE HUNDRED AND TWENTY ACRES, according to the County Clerk, is the extent of my worldly domain. But the County Clerk is a sleepy fellow, who never looks at his record books before nine o'clock. What they would show at daybreak is the question here at issue.

Books or no books, it is a fact, patent both to my dog and myself, that at daybreak I am the sole owner of all the acres I can walk over. It is not only boundaries that disappear, but also the thought of being bounded. Expanses unknown to deed or map are known to every dawn, and solitude, supposed no longer to exist in my county, extends on every hand as far as the dew can reach.

Like other great landowners, I have tenants. They are negligent about rents, but very punctilious about tenures. Indeed at every daybreak from April to July they proclaim their boundaries to each other, and so acknowledge, at least by inference, their fiefdom to me.

This daily ceremony, contrary to what you might suppose, begins with the utmost decorum. Who originally laid down its protocols I do not know. At 3:30 a.m., with such dignity as I can muster of a July morning, I step from my cabin door, bearing in either hand my emblems of sovereignty, a coffee pot and notebook. I seat myself on a bench, facing the white wake of the morning star. I set the pot beside me. I extract a cup from my shirt front, hoping none will notice its informal mode of transport. I get out my watch, pour coffee, and lay notebook on knee. This is the cue for the proclamations to begin.

The Shack, 3:30 a.m.

At 3:35 the nearest field sparrow avows, in a clear tenor chant, that he holds the jackpine copse north to the riverbank, and south to the old wagon track. One by one all the other field sparrows within earshot recite their respective holdings. There are no disputes, at least at this hour, so I just listen, hoping inwardly that their womenfolk acquiesce in this happy accord over the *status quo ante*.

Before the field sparrows have quite gone the rounds, the robin in the big elm warbles loudly his claim to the crotch where the icestorm tore off a limb, and all appurtenances pertaining thereto (meaning, in his case, all the angleworms in the not-very-spacious subjacent lawn).

The robin's insistent caroling awakens the oriole, who now tells the world of orioles that the pendant branch of the elm belongs to him, together with all fiber-bearing milkweed stalks near by, all loose strings in the garden, and the exclusive right to flash like a burst of fire from one of these to another.

My watch says 3:50. The indigo bunting on the hill asserts title to the dead oak limb left by the 1936 drought, and to divers near-by bugs and bushes. He does not claim, but I think he implies, the right to out-blue all bluebirds, and all spiderworts that have turned their faces to the dawn.

Next the wren—the one who discovered the knothole in the eave of the cabin— explodes into song. Half a dozen other wrens give voice, and now all is bedlam. Grosbeaks, thrashers, yellow warblers, bluebirds, vireos, towhees, cardinals—all are at it. My solemn list of performers, in their order and time of first song, hesitates, wavers, ceases, for my ear can no longer filter out priorities. Besides, the pot is empty and the sun is about to rise. I must inspect my domain before my title runs out.

Aldo's field essentials

We sally forth, the dog and I, at random. He has paid scant respect to all these vocal goings-on, for to him the evidence of tenancy is not song, but scent. Any illiterate bundle of feathers, he says, can make a noise in a tree. Now he is going to translate for me the olfactory poems that who-knows-what silent creatures have written in the summer night. At the end of each poem sits the author—if we can find him. What we actually find is beyond predicting: a rabbit, suddenly yearning to be elsewhere; a wood-cock, fluttering his disclaimer; a cock pheasant, indignant over wetting his feathers in the grass.

Once in a while we turn up a coon or mink, returning late from the night's foray. Sometimes we rout a heron from his unfinished fishing, or surprise a mother wood duck with her convoy of ducklings, headed full-steam for the shelter of the pickerelweeds. Sometimes we see deer sauntering back to the thickets, replete with alfalfa blooms, veronica, and wild lettuce. More often we see only the interweaving darkened lines that lazy hoofs have traced on the silken fabric of the dew.

I can feel the sun now. The bird-chorus has run out of breath. The far clank of cowbells bespeaks a herd ambling to pasture. A tractor roars warning that my neighbor is astir. The world has shrunk to those mean dimensions known to county clerks. We turn toward home, and breakfast.

White-tailed deer

Prairie Birthday

DURING EVERY WEEK FROM APRIL TO SEPTEMBER THERE ARE, on the average, ten wild plants coming into first bloom. In June as many as a dozen species may burst their buds on a single day. No man can heed all of these anniversaries; no man can ignore all of them. He who steps unseeing on May dandelions may be hauled up short by August ragweed pollen; he who ignores the ruddy haze of April elms may skid his car on the fallen corollas of June catalpas. Tell me of what plant-birthday a man takes notice, and I shall tell you a good deal about his vocation, his hobbies, his hay fever, and the general level of his ecological education.

❀   ❀   ❀

EVERY JULY I WATCH EAGERLY a certain country graveyard that I pass in driving to and from my farm. It is time for a prairie birthday, and in one corner of this graveyard lives a surviving celebrant of that once important event.

It is an ordinary graveyard, bordered by the usual spruces, and studded with the usual pink granite or white marble headstones, each with the usual Sunday bouquet of red or pink geraniums. It is extraordinary only in being triangular instead of square, and in harboring, within the sharp angle of its fence, a pin-point remnant of the native prairie on which the graveyard was established in the 1840's. Heretofore unreachable by scythe or mower, this yard-square relic of original Wisconsin gives birth, each July, to a man-high stalk of compass plant or cutleaf Silphium, spangled with saucer-sized yellow blooms resembling sunflowers. It is the sole remnant of this plant along this highway, and perhaps the sole remnant in the western half of our county. What a thousand acres of Silphiums looked like when they tickled the bellies of the buffalo is a question never again to be answered, and perhaps not even asked.

Compass plant, July

This year I found the Silphium in first bloom on 24 July, a week later than usual; during the last six years the average date was 15 July.

When I passed the graveyard again on 3 August, the fence had been removed by a road crew, and the Silphium cut. It is easy now to predict the future; for a few years my Silphium will try in vain to rise above the mowing machine, and then it will die. With it will die the prairie epoch.

The Highway Department says that 100,000 cars pass yearly over this route during the three summer months when the Silphium is in bloom. In them must ride at least 100,000 people who have "taken" what is called history, and perhaps 25,000 who have "taken" what is called botany. Yet I doubt whether a dozen have seen the Silphium, and of these hardly one will notice its demise. If I were to tell a preacher of the adjoining church that the road crew has been burning history books in his cemetery, under the guise of mowing weeds, he would be amazed and uncomprehending. How could a weed be a book?

This is one little episode in the funeral of the native flora, which in turn is one episode in the funeral of the floras of the world. Mechanized man, oblivious of floras, is proud of his progress in cleaning up the landscape on which, willy-nilly, he must live out his days. It might be wise to prohibit at once all teaching of real botany and real history, lest some future citizen suffer qualms about the floristic price of his good life.

᪊   ᪊   ᪊

THUS IT COMES TO PASS that farm neighborhoods are good in proportion to the poverty of their floras. My own farm was selected for its lack of goodness and its lack of highway; indeed my whole neighborhood lies in a backwash of the River Progress. My road is the original wagon track of the pioneers, innocent of grades or gravel, brushings or bulldozers. My neighbors bring a sigh to the County Agent. Their fencerows go unshaven for years on end. Their marshes are neither dyked nor drained. As between going fishing and going forward, they are prone to prefer fishing. Thus on week ends my floristic standard of living is that of the backwoods, while on week days I subsist as best I can on the flora of the university farms, the university campus, and the adjoining suburbs. For a decade I have kept, for pastime, a record of the wild plant species in first bloom on these two diverse areas:

Species First Blooming in	Suburb and Campus	Backward Farm
April	14	26
May	29	59
June	43	70
July	25	56
August	9	14
September	0	1
Total visual diet	120	226

It is apparent that the backward farmer's eye is nearly twice as well fed as the eye of the university student or businessman. Of course neither sees his flora as yet, so we are confronted by the two alternatives already mentioned: either insure the continued blindness of the populace, or examine the question whether we cannot have both progress and plants.

The shrinkage in the flora is due to a combination of clean-farming, woodlot grazing, and good roads. Each of these necessary changes of course requires a larger reduction in the acreage available for wild plants, but none of them requires, or benefits by, the erasure of species from whole farms, townships, or counties. There are idle spots on every farm, and every highway is bordered by an idle strip as long as it is; keep cow, plow, and mower out of these idle spots, and the full native flora, plus dozens of interesting stowaways from foreign parts, could be part of the normal environment of every citizen.

The outstanding conservator of the prairie flora, ironically enough, knows little and cares less about such frivolities: it is the railroad with its fenced right-of-way. Many of these railroad fences were erected before the prairie had been plowed. Within these linear reservations, oblivious of cinders, soot, and annual clean-up fires, the prairie flora still splashes its calendar of colors, from pink shooting-star in May to blue aster in October. I have long wished to confront some hard-boiled railway president with the physical evidence of his soft-heartedness. I have not done so because I haven't met one.

The railroads of course use flame-throwers and chemical sprays to clear the track of weeds, but the cost of such necessary clearance is still too high to extend it much beyond the actual rails. Perhaps further improvements are in the offing.

The erasure of a human subspecies is largely painless—to us—if we know little enough about it. A dead Chinaman is of little import to us whose awareness of things Chinese is bounded by an occasional dish of chow mein. We grieve only for what we know. The erasure of Silphium from western Dane County is no cause for grief if one knows it only as a name in a botany book.

Silphium first became a personality to me when I tried to dig one up to move to my farm. It was like digging an oak sapling. After half an hour of hot grimy labor the root was still enlarging, like a great vertical sweet-potato. As far as I know, that Silphium root went clear through to bedrock. I got no Silphium, but I learned by what elaborate underground stratagems it contrives to weather the prairie drouths.

Cone-flowers at sunset, Lissa's Prairie

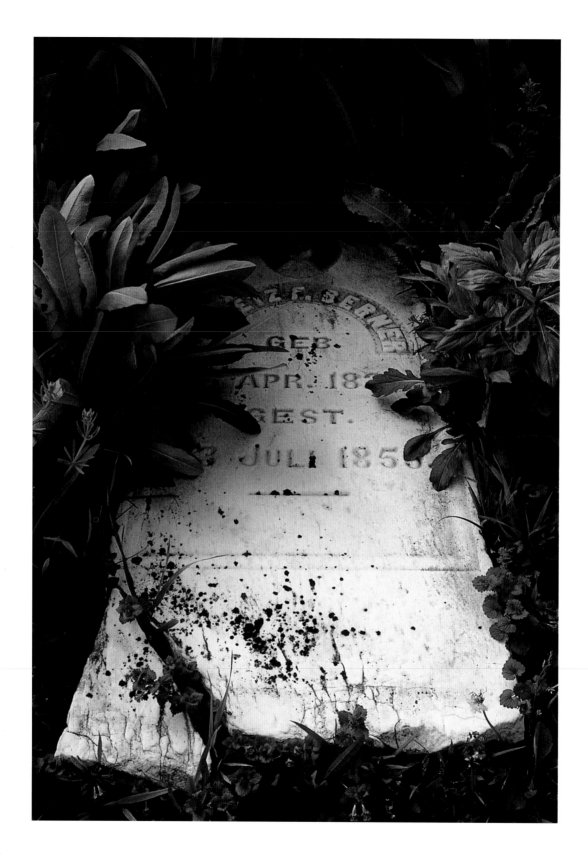

I next planted Silphium seeds, which are large, meaty, and taste like sunflower seeds. They came up promptly, but after five years of waiting the seedlings are still juvenile, and have not yet borne a flower-stalk. Perhaps it takes a decade for a Silphium to reach flowering age; how old, then, was my pet plant in the cemetery? It may have been older than the oldest tombstone, which is dated 1850. Perhaps it watched the fugitive Black Hawk retreat from the Madison lakes to the Wisconsin River; it stood on the route of that famous march. Certainly it saw the successive funerals of the local pioneers as they retired, one by one, to their repose beneath the bluestem.

I once saw a power shovel, while digging a roadside ditch, sever the "sweet-potato" root of a Silphium plant. The root soon sprouted new leaves, and eventually it again produced a flower stalk. This explains why this plant, which never invades new ground, is nevertheless sometimes seen on recently graded roadsides. Once established, it apparently withstands almost any kind of mutilation except continue grazing, mowing, or plowing.

Why does Silphium disappear from grazed areas? I once saw a farmer turn his cows into a virgin prairie meadow previously used only sporadically for mowing wild hay. The cows cropped the Silphium to the ground before any other plant was visibly eaten at all. One can imagine that the buffalo once had the same preference for Silphium, but he brooked no fences to confine his nibblings all summer long to one meadow. In short, the buffalo's pasturing was discontinuous, and therefore tolerable to Silphium.

It is a kind providence that has withheld a sense of history from the thousands of species of plants and animals that have exterminated each other to build the present world. The same kind providence now withholds it from us. Few grieved when the last buffalo left Wisconsin, and few will grieve when the last Silphium follows him to the lush prairies of the never-never land.

Tombstone, the cemetery

Following pages: prairie flowers in summer

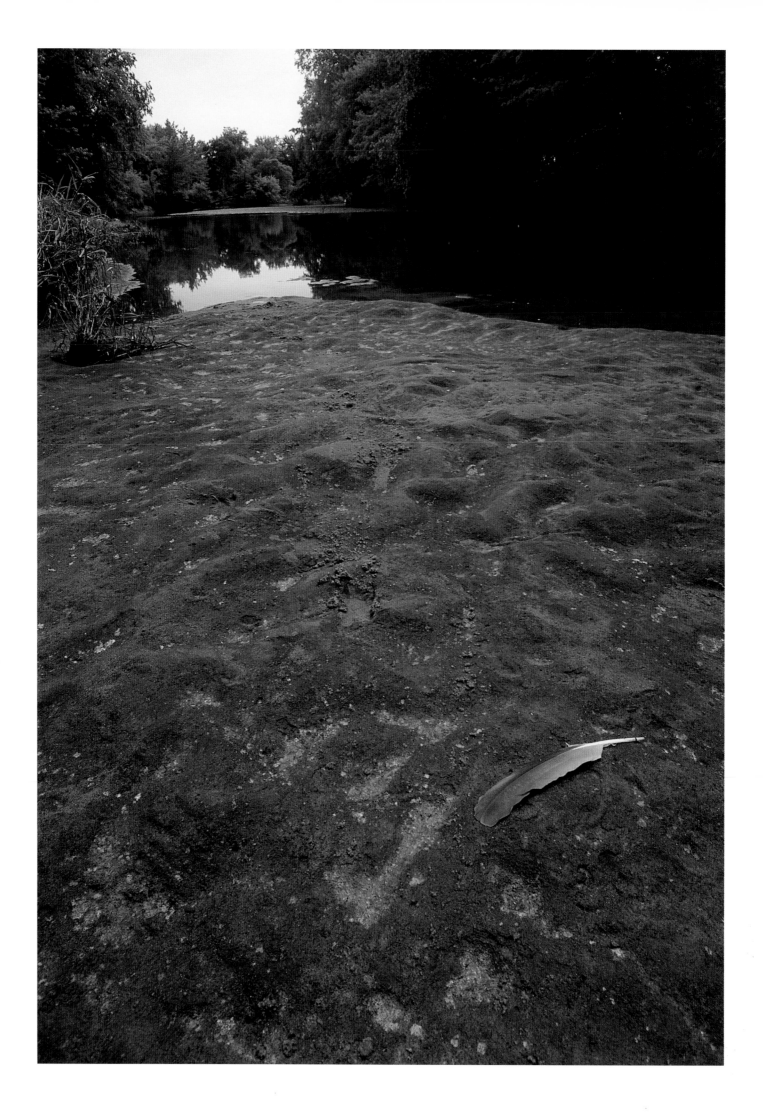

August

The Green Pasture

SOME PAINTINGS BECOME FAMOUS BECAUSE, being durable, they are viewed by successive generations, in each of which are likely to be found a few appreciative eyes.

I know a painting so evanescent that it is seldom viewed at all, except by some wandering deer. It is a river who wields the brush, and it is the same river who, before I can bring my friends to view his work, erases it forever from human view. After that it exists only in my mind's eye.

Like other artists, my river is temperamental; there is no predicting when the mood to paint will come upon him, or how long it will last. But in midsummer, when the great white fleets cruise the sky for day after flawless day, it is worth strolling down to the sandbars just to see whether he has been at work.

The work begins with a broad ribbon of silt brushed thinly on the sand of a receding shore. As this dries slowly in the sun, goldfinches bathe in its pools, and deer, herons, killdeers, raccoons, and turtles cover it with a lacework of tracks. There is no telling, at this stage, whether anything further will happen.

But when I see the silt ribbon turning green with Eleocharis, I watch closely thereafter, for this is the sign that the river is in a painting mood. Almost overnight the Eleocharis becomes a thick turf, so lush and so dense that the meadow mice from the adjoining upland cannot resist the temptation. They move *en masse* to the green pasture, and apparently spend the nights rubbing their ribs in its velvety depths. A maze of neatly tended mouse-trails bespeaks their enthusiasm. The deer walk up and down in it, apparently just for the pleasure of feeling it underfoot. Even a stay-at-home mole has tunneled his way across the dry bar to the Eleocharis ribbon, where he can heave and hump the verdant sod to his heart's content.

Sand bar and heron feather with deer tracks, the Wisconsin

At this stage the seedlings of plants too numerous to count and too young to recognize spring to life from the damp warm sand under the green ribbon.

To view the painting, give the river three more weeks of solitude, and then visit the bar on some bright morning just after the sun has melted the daybreak fog. The artist has now laid his colors, and sprayed them with dew. The Eleocharis sod, greener than ever, is now spangled with blue mimulus, pink dragon-head, and the milk-white blooms of Sagittaria. Here and there a cardinal flower thrusts a red spear skyward. At the head of the bar, purple ironweeds and pale pink joe-pyes stand tall against the wall of willows. And if you have come quietly and humbly, as you should to any spot that can be beautiful only once, you may surprise a fox-red deer, standing knee-high in the garden of his delight.

Do not return for a second view of the green pasture, for there is none. Either falling water has dried it out, or rising water has scoured the bar to its original austerity of clean sand. But in your mind you may hang up your picture, and hope that in some other summer the mood to paint may come upon the river.

Cardinal flower

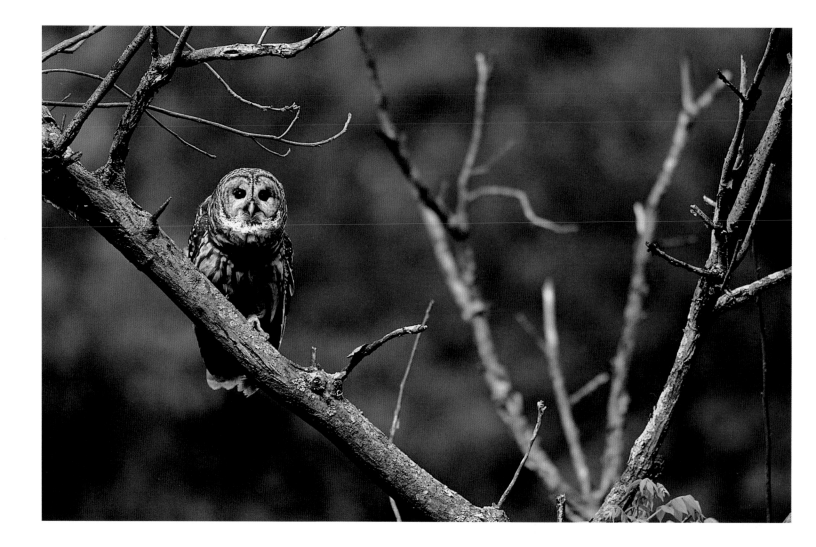

September

The Choral Copse

BY SEPTEMBER, the day breaks with little help from birds. A song sparrow may give a single half-hearted song, a woodcock may twitter overhead *en route* to his daytime thicket, a barred owl may terminate the night's argument with one last wavering call, but few other birds have anything to say or sing about.

It is on some, but not all, of these misty autumn daybreaks that one may hear the chorus of the quail. The silence is suddenly broken by a dozen contralto voices, no longer able to restrain their praise of the day to come. After a brief minute or two, the music closes as suddenly as it began.

Barred owl

Following pages: sunrise, the Great Marsh

There is a peculiar virtue in the music of elusive birds. Songsters that sing from top-most boughs are easily seen and as easily forgotten; they have the mediocrity of the obvious. What one remembers is the invisible hermit thrush pouring silver chords from impenetrable shadows; the soaring crane trumpeting from behind a cloud; the prairie chicken booming from the mists of nowhere; the quail's Ave Maria in the hush of dawn. No naturalist has even seen the choral act, for the covey is still on its invisible roost in the grass, and any attempt to approach automatically induces silence.

In June it is completely predictable that the robin will give voice when the light intensity reaches 0.01 candle power, and that the bedlam of other singers will follow in predictable sequence. In autumn, on the other hand, the robin is silent, and it is quite unpredictable whether the covey-chorus will occur at all. The disappointment I feel on these mornings of silence perhaps shows that things hoped for have a higher value than things assured. The hope of hearing quail is worth half a dozen risings-in-the-dark.

My farm always has one or more coveys in autumn, but the daybreak chorus is usually distant. I think this is because the coveys prefer to roost as far as possible from the dog, whose interest in quail is even more ardent than my own. One October dawn, however, as I sat sipping coffee by the outdoor fire, a chorus burst into song hardly a stone's throw away. They had roosted under a white-pine copse, possibly to stay dry during the heavy dews.

We felt honored by this daybreak hymn sung almost at our doorstep. Somehow the blue autumnal needles on those pines became thenceforth bluer, and the red carpet of dewberry under those pines became even redder.

Sandhill cranes

October

Smoky Gold

THERE ARE TWO KINDS OF HUNTING: ordinary hunting, and ruffed-grouse hunting.

There are two places to hunt grouse: ordinary places, and Adams County.

There are two times to hunt in Adams: ordinary times, and when the tamaracks are smoky gold. This is written for those luckless ones who have never stood, gun empty and mouth agape, to watch the golden needles come sifting down, while the feathery rocket that knocked them off sails unscathed into the jackpines.

The tamaracks change from green to yellow when the first frosts have brought woodcock, fox sparrows, and juncos out of the north. Troops of robins are stripping the last white berries from the dogwood thickets, leaving the empty stems as a pink haze against the hill. The creekside alders have shed their leaves, exposing here and there an eyeful of holly. Brambles are aglow, lighting your footsteps grouseward.

The dog knows what is grouseward better than you do. You will do well to follow him closely, reading from the cock of his ears the story the breeze is telling. When at last he stops stock-still, and says with a sideward glance, "Well, get ready," the question is, ready for what? A twittering woodcock, or the rising roar of a grouse, or perhaps only a rabbit? In this moment of uncertainty is condensed much of the virtue of grouse hunting. He who must know what to get ready for should go and hunt pheasants.

October tamaracks

HUNTS DIFFER IN FLAVOR, but the reasons are subtle. The sweetest hunts are stolen. To steal a hunt, either go far into the wilderness where no one has been, or else find some undiscovered place under everybody's nose.

Few hunters know that grouse exist in Adams County, for when they drive through it, they see only a waste of jackpines and scrub oaks. This is because the highway intersects a series of west-running creeks, each of which heads in a swamp, but drops to the river through dry sand-barrens. Naturally the northbound highway intersects these swampless barrens, but just above the highway, and behind the screen of dry scrub, every creeklet expands into a broad ribbon of swamp, a sure haven for grouse.

Here, come October, I sit in the solitude of my tamaracks and hear the hunters' cars roaring up the highway, hell-bent for the crowded counties to the north. I chuckle as I picture their dancing speedometers, their strained faces, their eager eyes glued on the northward horizon. At the noise of their passing, a cock grouse drums his defiance. My dog grins as we note his direction. That fellow, we agree, needs some exercise; we shall look him up presently.

The tamaracks grow not only in the swamp, but at the foot of the bordering upland, where springs break forth. Each spring has become choked with moss, which forms a boggy terrace. I call these terraces the hanging gardens, for out of their sodden muck the fringed gentians have lifted blue jewels. Such an October gentian, dusted with tamarack gold, is worth a full stop and a long look, even when the dog signals grouse ahead.

Between each hanging garden and the creekside is a moss-paved deer trail, handy for the hunter to follow, and for the flushed grouse to cross—in a split second. The question is whether the bird and the gun agree on how a second should be split. If they do not, the next deer that passes finds a pair of empty shells to sniff at, but no feathers.

Lily pads, Chapman Lake

Higher up the creeklet I encounter an abandoned farm. I try to read, from the age of the young jackpines marching across an old field, how long ago the luckless farmer found out that sand plains were meant to grow solitude, not corn. Jackpines tell tall tales to the unwary, for they put on several whorls of branches each year, instead of only one. I find a better chronometer in an elm seedling that now blocks the barn door. Its rings date back to the drouth of 1930. Since that year no man has carried milk out of this barn.

I wonder what this family thought about when their mortgage finally outgrew their crops, and thus gave the signal for their eviction. Many thoughts, like flying grouse, leave no trace of their passing, but some leave clues that outlast the decades. He who, in some unforgotten April, planted this lilac must have thought pleasantly of blooms for all the Aprils to come. She who used this washboard, its corrugations worn thin with many Mondays, may have wished for a cessation of all Mondays, and soon.

Abandoned farmhouse

Musing on such questions, I become aware of the dog down by the spring, pointing patiently these many minutes. I walk up, apologizing for my inattention. Up twitters a woodcock, batlike, his salmon breast soaked in October sun. Thus goes the hunt.

It's hard on such a day to keep one's mind on grouse, for there are many distractions. I cross a buck track in the sand, and follow in idle curiosity. The track leads straight from one Jersey tea bush to another, with nipped twigs showing why.

This reminds me of my own lunch, but before I get it pulled out of my game pocket, I see a circling hawk, high skyward, needing identification. I wait till he banks and shows his red tail.

I reach again for the lunch, but my eye catches a peeled popple. Here a buck has rubbed off his itchy velvet. How long ago? The exposed wood is already brown; I conclude that horns must therefore be clean by now.

I reach again for the lunch, but am interrupted by an excited yawp from the dog, and a crash of bushes in the swamp. Out springs a buck, flag aloft, horns shining, his coat a sleek blue. Yes, the popple told the truth.

This time I get the lunch all the way out and sit down to eat. A chickadee watches me, and grows confidential about his lunch. He doesn't say what he ate, perhaps it was cool turgid ant-eggs, or some other avian equivalent of cold roast grouse.

Lunch over, I regard a phalanx of young tamaracks, their golden lances thrusting skyward. Under each the needles of yesterday fall to earth building a blanket of smoky gold; at the tip of each the bud of tomorrow, preformed, poised, awaits another spring.

White-tailed buck, Sedge Meadow

Too Early

GETTING UP TOO EARLY is a vice habitual in horned owls, stars, geese, and freight trains. Some hunters acquire it from geese, and some coffee pots from hunters. It is strange that of all the multitude of creatures who must rise in the morning at some time, only these few should have discovered the most pleasant and least useful time for doing it.

Orion must have been the original mentor of the too-early company, for it is he who signals for too-early rising. It is time when Orion has passed west of the zenith about as far as one should lead a teal.

Early risers feel at ease with each other, perhaps because, unlike those who sleep late, they are given to understatement of their own achievements. Orion, the most widely traveled, says literally nothing. The coffee pot, from its first soft gurgle, underclaims the virtues of what simmers within. The owl, in his trisyllabic commentary, plays down the story of the night's murders. The goose on the bar, rising briefly to a point of order in some inaudible anserine debate, lets fall no hint that he speaks with the authority of all the far hills and the sea.

The freight, I admit, is hardly reticent about his own importance, yet even he has a kind of modesty: his eye is single to his own noisy business, and he never comes roaring into somebody else's camp. I feel a deep security in this single-mindedness of freight trains.

❦   ❦   ❦

TO ARRIVE TOO EARLY in the marsh is an adventure in pure listening; the ear roams at will among the noises of the night, without let or hindrance from hand or eye. When you hear a mallard being audibly enthusiastic about his soup, you are free to picture a score guzzling among the duckweeds. When one widgeon squeals, you may postulate a squadron without fear of visual contradiction. And when a flock of bluebills, pitching pondward, tears the dark silk of heaven in one long rending nose-dive, you catch your breath at the sound, but there is nothing to see except stars. This same performance, in daytime, would have to be looked at, shot at, missed, and then hurriedly fitted with an alibi. Nor could daylight add anything to your mind's eye picture of quivering wings, ripping the firmament neatly into halves.

Geese, pre-dawn

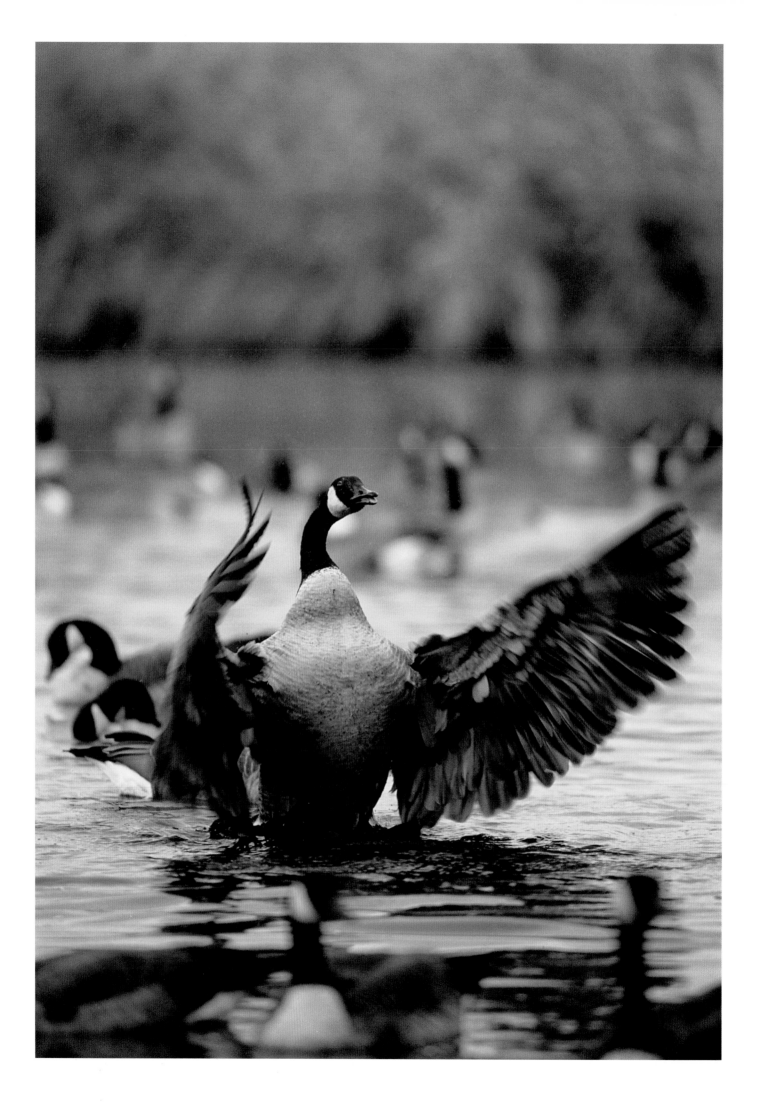

The hour of listening ends when the fowl depart on muted wings for wider safer waters, each flock a blur against the graying east.

Like many another treaty of restraint, the pre-dawn pact lasts only as long as darkness humbles the arrogant. It would seem as if the sun were responsible for the daily retreat of reticence from the world. At any rate, by the time the mists are white over the lowlands, every rooster is bragging *ad lib*, and every corn shock is pretending to be twice as tall as any corn that ever grew. By sun-up every squirrel is exaggerating some fancied indignity to his person, and every jay proclaiming with false emotion about suppositious dangers to society, at this very moment discovered by him. Distant crows are berating a hypothetical owl, just to tell the world how vigilant crows are, and a pheasant cock, musing perhaps on his philanderings of bygone days, beats the air with his wings and tells the world in raucous warning that he owns this marsh and all the hens in it.

Nor are all these illusions of grandeur confined to the birds and beasts. By break-fast time come the honks, horns, shouts, and whistles of the awakened farmyard, and finally, at evening, the drone of an untended radio. Then everybody goes to bed to relearn the lessons of the night.

Canada goose, the Great Marsh

Following pages: Aldo's woods from the Great Marsh

Red Lanterns

ONE WAY TO HUNT PARTRIDGE is to make a plan, based on logic and probabilities, of the terrain to be hunted. This will take you over the ground where the birds ought to be.

Another way is to wander, quite aimlessly, from one red lantern to another. This will likely take you where the birds actually are. The lanterns are blackberry leaves, red in October sun.

Red lanterns have lighted my way on many a pleasant hunt in many a region, but I think that blackberries must first have learned how to glow in the sand counties of central Wisconsin. Along the little boggy streams of these friendly wastes, called poor by those whose own lights barely flicker, the blackberries burn richly red on every sunny day from first frost to the last day of the season. Every woodcock and every partridge has his private solarium under these briars. Most hunters, not knowing this, wear themselves out in the briarless scrub, and, returning home birdless, leave the rest of us in peace.

By "us" I mean the birds, the stream, the dog, and myself. The stream is a lazy one; he winds through the alders as if he would rather stay here than reach the river. So would I. Every one of his hairpin hesitations means that much more streambank where hillside briars adjoin dank beds of frozen ferns and jewelweeds on the boggy bottom. No partridge can long absent himself from such a place, nor can I. Partridge hunting, then, is a creekside stroll, upwind, from one briar patch to another.

Blackberry leaves

The dog, when he approaches the briars, looks around to make sure I am within gunshot. Reassured, he advances with stealthy caution, his wet nose screening a hundred scents for that one scent, the potential presence of which gives life and meaning to the whole landscape. He is the prospector of the air, perpetually searching its strata for olfactory gold. Partridge scent is the gold standard that relates his world to mine.

My dog, by the way, thinks I have much to learn about partridges, and, being a professional naturalist, I agree. He persists in tutoring me, with the calm patience of a professor of logic, in the art of drawing deductions from an educated nose. I delight in seeing him deduce a conclusion, in the form of a point, from data that are obvious to him, but speculative to my unaided eye. Perhaps he hopes his dull pupil will one day learn to smell.

Like other dull pupils, I know when the professor is right, even though I do not know why. I check my gun and walk in. Like any good professor, the dog never laughs when I miss, which is often. He gives me just one look, and proceeds up the stream in quest of another grouse.

Following one of these banks, one walks astride two landscapes, the hillside one hunts from, and the bottom the dog hunts in. There is a special charm in treading soft dry carpets of Lycopodium to flush birds out of the bog, and the first test of a partridge dog is his willingness to do the wet work while you parallel him on the dry bank.

A special problem arises where the belt of alders widens, and the dog disappears from view. Hurry at once to a knoll or point, where you stand stock-still, straining eye and ear to follow the dog. A sudden scattering of whitethroats may reveal his whereabouts. Again you may hear him breaking a twig, or splashing in a wet spot, or plopping into the creek. But when all sound ceases, be ready for instant action, for he is likely on point. Listen now for the premonitory clucks a frightened partridge gives just before flushing. Then follows the hurtling bird, or perhaps two of them, or I have known as many as six, clucking and flushing one by one, each sailing high for his own destination in the uplands. Whether one passes within gunshot is of course a matter of chance, and you can compute the chance if you have time: 360 degrees divided by 30, or whatever segment of the circle your gun covers. Divide again by 3 or 4, which is your chance of missing, and you have the probability of actual feathers in the hunting coat.

Path through blackberries

The second test of a good partridge dog is whether he reports for orders after such an episode. Sit down and talk it over with him while he pants. Then look for the next red lantern, and proceed with the hunt.

The October breeze brings my dog many scents other than grouse, each of which may lead to its own peculiar episode. When he points with a certain humorous expression of the ears, I know he has found a bedded rabbit. Once a dead-serious point yielded no bird, but still the dog stood frozen; in a tuft of sedge under his very nose was a fat sleeping coon, getting his share of October sun. At least once on each hunt the dog bays a skunk, usually in some denser-than-ordinary thicket of blackberries. Once the dog pointed in midstream: a whir of wings upriver, followed by three musical cries, told me he had interrupted a wood duck's dinner. Not infrequently he finds jacksnipe in heavily pastured alders, and lastly he may put out a deer, bedded for the day on a high streambank flanked by alder bog. Has the deer a poetical weakness for singing waters, or a practical liking for a bed that cannot be approached without making a noise? Judging by the indignant flick of his great white flag it might be either, or both.

Almost anything may happen between one red lantern and another.

§   §   §

AT SUNSET ON THE LAST DAY OF THE GROUSE SEASON, every blackberry blows out his light. I do not understand how a mere bush can thus be infallibly informed about the Wisconsin statutes, nor have I ever gone back next day to find out. For the ensuing eleven months the lanterns glow only in recollection. I sometimes think that the other months were constituted mainly as a fitting interlude between Octobers, and I suspect that dogs, and perhaps grouse, share the same view.

Treed opossum

November

If I Were the Wind

THE WIND THAT MAKES MUSIC IN NOVEMBER CORN is in a hurry. The stalks hum, the loose husks whisk skyward in half-playful swirls, and the wind hurries on.

In the marsh, long windy waves surge across the grassy sloughs, beat against the far willows. A tree tries to argue, bare limbs waving, but there is no detaining the wind.

On the sandbar there is only wind, and the river sliding seaward. Every wisp of grass is drawing circles on the sand. I wander over the bar to a driftwood log, where I sit and listen to the universal roar, and to the tinkle of wavelets on the shore. The river is lifeless: not a duck, heron, marshhawk, or gull but has sought refuge from wind.

❧ ❧ ❧

OUT OF THE CLOUDS I HEAR A FAINT BARK, as of a far-away dog. It is strange how the world cocks its ears at that sound, wondering. Soon it is louder: the honk of geese, invisible, but coming on.

The flock emerges from the low clouds, a tattered banner of birds, dipping and rising, blown up and blown down, blown together and blown apart, but advancing, the wind wrestling lovingly with each winnowing wing. When the flock is a blur in the far sky I hear the last honk, sounding taps for summer.

❧ ❧ ❧

IT IS WARM BEHIND THE DRIFTWOOD NOW, for the wind has gone with the geese. So would I—if I were the wind.

Windblown geese

Axe-in-Hand

THE LORD GIVETH, and the Lord taketh away, but He is no longer the only one to do so. When some remote ancestor of ours invented the shovel, he became a giver: he could plant a tree. And when the axe was invented, he became a taker: he could chop it down. Whoever owns land has thus assumed, whether he knows it or not, the divine functions of creating and destroying plants.

Other ancestors, less remote, have since invented other tools, but each of these, upon close scrutiny, proves to be either an elaboration of, or an accessory to, the original pair of basic implements. We classify ourselves into vocations, each of which either wields some particular tool, or sells it, or repairs it, or sharpens it, or dispenses advice on how to do so; by such division of labors we avoid responsibility for the misuse of any tool save our own. But there is one vocation—philosophy—which knows that all men, by what they think about and wish for, in effect wield all tools. It knows that men thus determine, by their manner of thinking and wishing, whether it is worth while to wield any.

Aldo's axe-grinding wheel, the farm

NOVEMBER IS, for many reasons, the month for the axe. It is warm enough to grind an axe without freezing, but cold enough to fell a tree in comfort. The leaves are off the hardwoods, so that one can see just how the branches intertwine, and what growth occurred last summer. Without this clear view of treetops, one cannot be sure which tree, if any, needs felling for the good of the land.

I have read many definitions of what is a conservationist, and written not a few myself, but I suspect that the best one is written not with a pen, but with an axe. It is a matter of what a man thinks about while chopping, or while deciding what to chop. A conservationist is one who is humbly aware that with each stroke he is writing his signature on the face of his land. Signatures of course differ, whether written with axe or pen, and this is as it should be.

Leafless branches at sunrise

I find it disconcerting to analyze, *ex post facto*, the reasons behind my own axe-in-hand decisions. I find, first of all, that not all trees are created free and equal. Where a white pine and a red birch are crowding each other, I have an *a priori* bias; I always cut the birch to favor the pine. Why?

Well, first of all, I planted the pine with my shovel, whereas the birch crawled in under the fence and planted itself. My bias is thus to some extent paternal, but this cannot be the whole story, for if the pine were a natural seedling like the birch, I would value it even more. So I must dig deeper for the logic, if any, behind my bias.

The birch is an abundant tree in my township and becoming more so, whereas pine is scarce and becoming scarcer; perhaps my bias is for the underdog. But what would I do if my farm were further north, where pine is abundant and red birch is scarce? I confess I don't know. My farm is here.

The pine will live for a century, the birch for half that; do I fear that my signature will fade? My neighbors have planted no pines but all have many birches; am I snobbish about having a woodlot of distinction? The pine stays green all winter, the birch punches the clock in October; do I favor the tree that, like myself, braves the winter wind? The pine will shelter a grouse but the birch will feed him; do I consider bed more important than board? The pine will ultimately bring ten dollars a thousand, the birch two dollars; have I an eye on the bank? All of these possible reasons for my bias seem to carry some weight, but none of them carries very much.

So I try again, and here perhaps is something; under this pine will ultimately grow a trailing arbutus, an Indian pipe, a pyrola, or a twin flower, whereas under the birch a bottle gentian is about the best to be hoped for. In this pine a pileated woodpecker will ultimately chisel out a nest; in the birch a hairy will have to suffice. In this pine the wind will sing for me in April, at which time the birch is only rattling naked twigs. These possible reasons for my bias carry weight, but why? Does the pine stimulate my imagination and my hopes more deeply than the birch does? If so, is the difference in the trees, or in me?

The only conclusion I have ever reached is that I love all trees, but I am in love with pines.

As I said, November is the month for the axe, and, as in other love affairs, there is skill in the exercise of bias. If the birch stands south of the pine, and is taller, it will shade the pine's leader in the spring, and thus discourage the pine weevil from laying her eggs there. Birch competition is a minor affliction compared with this weevil, whose progeny kill the pine's leader and thus deform the tree. It is interesting to meditate that this insect's preference for squatting in the sun determines not only her own continuity as a species, but also the future figure of my pine, and my own success as a wielder of axe and shovel.

Again, if a drouthy summer follows my removal of the birch's shade, the hotter soil may offset the lesser competition for water, and my pine be none the better for my bias.

Lastly, if the birch's limbs rub the pine's terminal buds during a wind, the pine will surely be deformed, and the birch must either be removed regardless of other considerations, or else it must be pruned of limbs each winter to a height greater than the pine's prospective summer growth.

Such are the pros and cons the wielder of an axe must foresee, compare, and decide upon with the calm assurance that his bias will, on the average, prove to be something more than good intentions.

The wielder of an axe has as many biases as there are species of trees on his farm. In the course of the years he imputes to each species, from his responses to their beauty or utility, and their responses to his labors for or against them, a series of attributes that constitute a character. I am amazed to learn what diverse characters different men impute to one and the same tree.

Thus to me the aspen is in good repute because he glorifies October and he feeds my grouse in winter, but to some of my neighbors he is a mere weed, perhaps because he sprouted so vigorously in the stump lots their grandfathers were attempting to clear. (I cannot sneer at this, for I find myself disliking the elms whose resproutings threaten my pines.)

Again, the tamarack is to me a favorite second only to white pine, perhaps because he is nearly extinct in my township (underdog bias), or because he sprinkles gold on October grouse (gunpowder bias), or because he sours the soil and enables it to grow the loveliest of our orchids, the showy lady's-slipper. On the other hand, foresters have excommunicated the tamarack because he grows too slowly to pay compound interest. In order to clinch this dispute, they also mention that he succumbs periodically to epizootics of saw-fly, but this is fifty years hence for my tamaracks, so I shall let my grandson worry about it. Meanwhile my tamaracks are growing so lustily that my spirits soar with them, skyward.

To me an ancient cottonwood is the greatest of trees because in his youth he shaded the buffalo and wore a halo of pigeons, and I like a young cottonwood because he may some day become ancient. But the farmer's wife (and hence the farmer) despises all cottonwoods because in June the female tree clogs the screens with cotton. The modern dogma is comfort at any cost.

I find my biases more numerous than those of my neighbors because I have individual likings for many species that they lump under one aspersive category: brush. Thus I like the wahoo, partly because deer, rabbits, and mice are so avid to eat his square twigs and green bark and partly because his cerise berries glow so warmly against November snow. I like the red dogwood because he feeds October robins, and the prickly ash because my woodcock take their daily sunbath under the shelter of his thorns. I like the hazel because his October purple feeds my eye, and because his November catkins feed my deer and grouse. I like the bittersweet because my father did, and because the deer, on the 1st of July of each year, begin suddenly to eat the new leaves, and I have learned to predict this event to my guests. I cannot dislike a plant that enables me, a mere professor, to blossom forth annually as a successful seer and prophet.

It is evident that our plant biases are in part traditional. If your grandfather liked hickory nuts, you will like the hickory tree because your father told you to. If, on the other hand, your grandfather burned a log carrying a poison ivy vine and recklessly stood in the smoke, you will dislike the species, no matter with what crimson glories it warms your eyes each fall.

It is also evident that our plant biases reflect not only vocations but avocations, with a delicate allocation of priority as between industry and indolence. The farmer who would-rather hunt grouse than milk cows will not dislike hawthorn, no matter if it does invade his pasture. The coon-hunter will not dislike basswood, and I know of quail hunters who bear no grudge against ragweed, despite their annual bout with hayfever. Our biases are indeed a sensitive index to our affections, our tastes, our loyalties, our generosities, and our manner of wasting weekends.

Be that as it may, I am content to waste mine, in November, with axe in hand.

Bluebird and dogwood berries

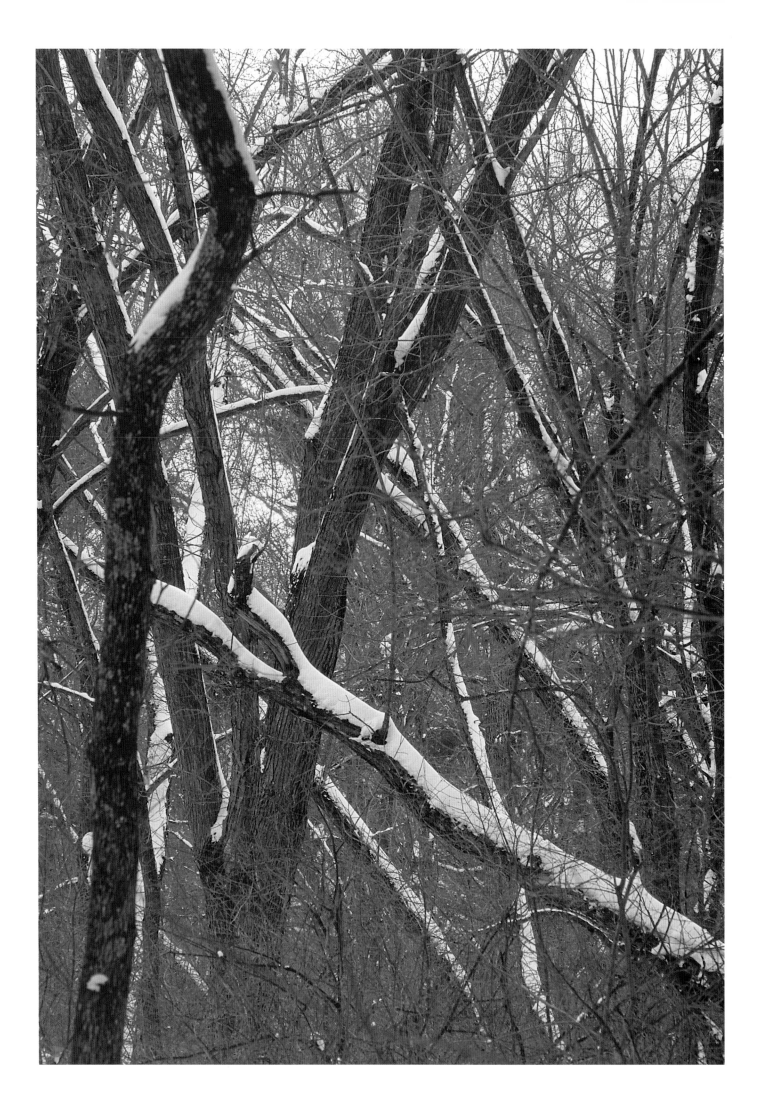

A Mighty Fortress

EVERY FARM WOODLAND, in addition to yielding lumber, fuel, and posts, should provide its owner a liberal education. This crop of wisdom never fails, but it is not always harvested. I here record some of the many lessons I have learned in my own woods.

※   ※   ※

SOON AFTER I BOUGHT THE WOODS a decade ago, I realized that I had bought almost as many tree diseases as I had trees. My woodlot is riddled by all the ailments wood is heir to. I began to wish that Noah, when he loaded up the Ark, had left the tree diseases behind. But it soon became clear that these same diseases made my woodlot a mighty fortress, unequaled in the whole county.

My woods is headquarters for a family of coons; few of my neighbors have any. One Sunday in November, after a new snow, I learned why. The fresh track of a coon-hunter and his hound led up to a half-uprooted maple, under which one of my coons had taken refuge. The frozen snarl of roots and earth was too rocky to chop and too tough to dig; the holes under the roots were too numerous to smoke out. The hunter had quit coonless because a fungus disease had weakened the roots of the maple. The tree, half tipped over by a storm, offers an impregnable fortress for coondom. Without this "bombproof" shelter, my seed stock of coons would be cleaned out by hunters each year.

My woods houses a dozen ruffed grouse, but during periods of deep snow my grouse shift to my neighbor's woods, where there is better cover. However, I always retain as many grouse as I have oaks wind-thrown by summer storms. These summer windfalls keep their dried leaves, and during snows each such windfall harbors a grouse. The droppings show that each grouse roosts, feeds, and loafs for the duration of the storm within the narrow confines of his leafy camouflage, safe from wind, owl, fox, and hunter. The cured oak leaves not only serve as cover, but, for some curious reason, are relished as food by the grouse.

These oak windfalls are, of course, diseased trees. Without disease, few oaks would break off, and hence few grouse would have down tops to hide in.

Sunset, Aldo's woods

Diseased oaks also provide another apparently delectable grouse food: oak galls. A gall is a diseased growth of new twigs that have been stung by a gall-wasp while tender and succulent. In October my grouse are often stuffed with oak galls.

Each year the wild bees load up one of my hollow oaks with combs, and each year trespassing honey-hunters harvest the honey before I do. This is partly because they are more skillful than I am in "lining up" the bee trees, and partly because they use nets, and hence are able to work before the bees become dormant in fall. But for heart-rots, there would be no hollow oaks to furnish wild bees with oaken hives.

During high years of the cycle, there is a plague of rabbits in my woods. They eat the bark and twigs off almost every kind of tree or bush I am trying to encourage, and ignore almost every kind I should like to have less of. (When the rabbit-hunter plants himself a grove of pines or an orchard, the rabbit somehow ceases to be a game animal and becomes a pest instead.)

The rabbit, despite his omnivorous appetite, is an epicure in some respects. He always prefers a hand-planted pine, maple, apple, or wahoo to a wild one. He also insists that certain salads be preconditioned before he deigns to eat them. Thus he spurns red dogwood until it is attacked by oyster-shell scale, after which the bark becomes a delicacy, to be eagerly devoured by all the rabbits in the neighborhood.

A flock of a dozen chickadees spends the year in my woods. In winter, when we are harvesting diseased or dead trees for our fuel wood, the ring of the axe is dinner gong for the chickadee tribe. They hang in the offing waiting for the tree to fall, offering pert commentary on the slowness of our labor. When the tree at last is down, and the wedges begin to open up its contents, the chickadees draw up their white napkins and fall to. Every slab of dead bark is, to them, a treasury of eggs, larvae, and cocoons. For them every ant-tunneled heartwood bulges with milk and honey. We often stand a fresh split against a near-by tree just to see the greedy chicks mop up the ant-eggs. It lightens our labor to know that they, as well as we, derive aid and comfort from the fragrant riches of newly split oak.

But for diseases and insect pests, there would likely be no food in these trees, and hence no chickadees to add cheer to my woods in winter.

Wild bees

Many other kinds of wildlife depend on tree diseases. My pileated woodpeckers chisel living pines, to extract fat grubs from the diseased heartwood. My barred owls find surcease from crows and jays in the hollow heart of an old basswood; but for this diseased tree their sundown serenade would probably be silenced. My wood ducks nest in hollow trees; every June brings its brood of downy ducklings to my woodland slough. All squirrels depend, for permanent dens, on a delicately balanced equilibrium between a rotting cavity and the scar tissue with which the tree attempts to close the wound. The squirrels referee the contest by gnawing out the scar tissue when it begins unduly to shrink the amplitude of their front door.

The real jewel of my disease-ridden woodlot is the prothonotary warbler. He nests in an old woodpecker hole, or other small cavity, in a dead snag overhanging water. The flash of his gold-and-blue plumage amid the dank decay of the June woods is in itself proof that dead trees are transmuted into living animals, and vice versa. When you doubt the wisdom of this arrangement, take a look at the prothonotary.

Pileated woodpecker

December

Home Range

THE WILD THINGS THAT LIVE ON MY FARM ARE RELUCTANT TO TELL ME, in so many words, how much of my township is included within their daily or nightly beat. I am curious about this, for it gives me the ratio between the size of their universe and the size of mine, and it conveniently begs the much more important question, who is the more thoroughly acquainted with the world in which he lives?

Like people, my animals frequently disclose by their actions what they decline to divulge in words. It is difficult to predict when and how one of these disclosures will come to light.

❦   ❦   ❦

THE DOG, being no hand with an axe, is free to hunt while the rest of us are making wood. A sudden *yip-yip-yip* gives us notice that a rabbit, flushed from his bed in the grass, is headed elsewhere in a hurry. He makes a beeline for a woodpile a quarter-mile distant, where he ducks between two corded stacks, a safe gunshot ahead of his pursuer. The dog, after leaving a few symbolic toothmarks on the hard oak, gives it up and resumes his search for some less canny cottontail, and we resume our chopping.

This little episode tells me that this rabbit is familiar with all of the ground between his bed in the meadow and his blitz-cellar under the woodpile. How else the beeline? This rabbit's home range is at least a quarter-mile in extent.

The chickadees that visit our feeding station are trapped and banded each winter. Some of our neighbors also feed chickadees, but none band them. By noticing the furthest points from my feeder at which banded chickadees are seen, we have learned that the home range of our flock is half a mile across in winter, but that it includes only areas protected from wind.

In summer, when the flock has dispersed for nesting, banded birds are seen at greater distances, often mated with unbanded birds. At this season the chickadees pay no heed to wind, often being found in open wind-swept places.

Animal tracks around the Shack

The fresh tracks of three deer, clear in yesterday's snow, pass through our woods. I follow the tracks backward and find a cluster of three beds, clear of snow, in the big willow thicket on the sandbar.

I then follow the tracks forward; they lead to my neighbor's cornfield, where the deer have pawed waste corn out of the snow, and also tousled one of the shocks. The tracks then lead back, by another route, to the sandbar. *En route* the deer have pawed at some grass tufts, nuzzling for the tender green sprouts within, and they have also drunk at a spring. My picture of the night's routine is complete. The over-all distance from bed to breakfast is a mile.

Our woods always harbors grouse, but one day last winter, after a deep and soft snow, I could find neither a grouse nor a track of one. I had about concluded that my birds had moved out, when my dog came to a point in the leafy top of an oak blown down last summer. Three grouse flushed out, one by one.

There were no tracks under or near the down top. Obviously these birds had flown in, but from where? Grouse must eat, especially in zero weather, so I examined the droppings for a clue. Among much unrecognizable debris I found bud-scales, and also the tough yellow skins of frozen nightshade berries.

In a thicket of young soft maple I had noticed, in summer, an abundant growth of nightshade. I went there and, after a search, found grouse tracks on a log. The birds had not waded the soft snow; they had walked the logs and picked the berries projecting here and there within their reach. This was a quarter-mile east of the down oak.

That evening, at sunset, I saw a grouse budding in a popple thicket a quarter-mile west. There were no tracks. This completed the story. These birds, for the duration of the soft snow, were covering their home range a-wing, not afoot, and the range was half a mile across.

※   ※   ※

SCIENCE KNOWS LITTLE ABOUT HOME RANGE: how big it is at various seasons, what food and cover it must include, when and how it is defended against trespass, and whether ownership is an individual, family, or group affair. These are the fundamentals of animal economics, or ecology. Every farm is a textbook on animal ecology; woodsmanship is the translation of the book.

Deer tracks, cornfield

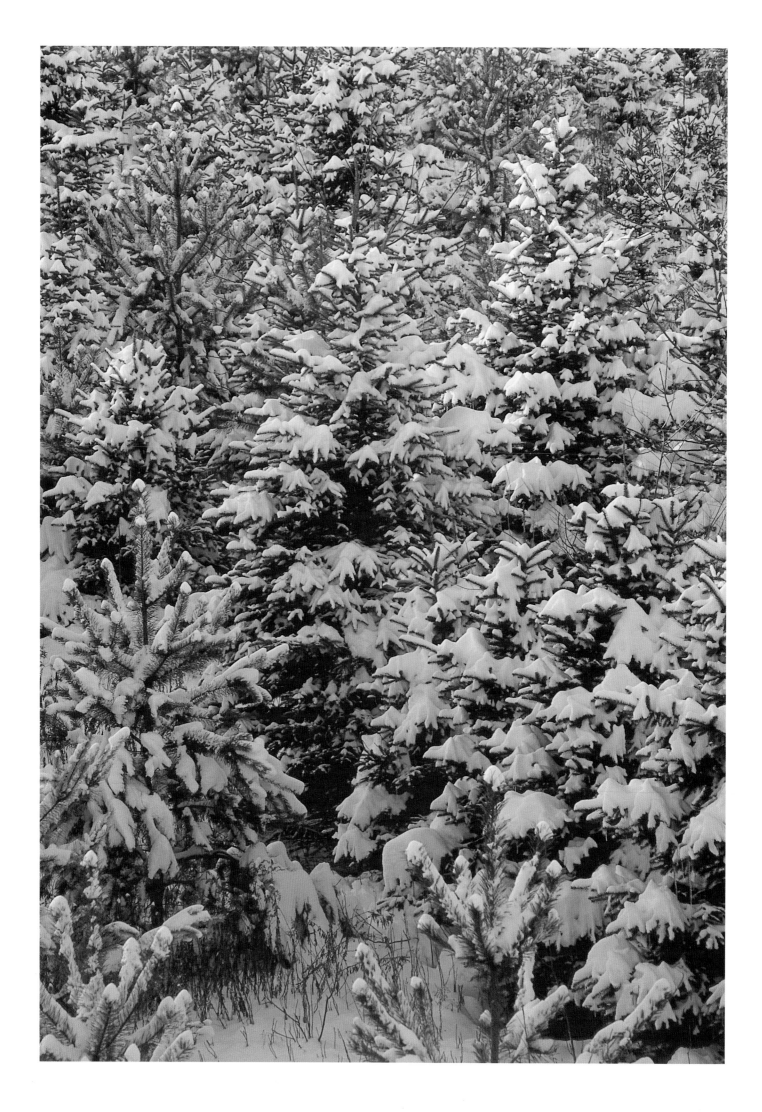

Pines above the Snow

ACTS OF CREATION ARE ORDINARILY RESERVED FOR GODS AND POETS, but humbler folk may circumvent this restriction if they know how. To plant a pine, for example, one need be neither god nor poet; one need only own a shovel. By virtue of this curious loophole in the rules, any clodhopper may say: Let there be a tree—and there will be one.

If his back be strong and his shovel sharp, there may eventually be ten thousand. And in the seventh year he may lean upon his shovel, and look upon his trees, and find them good.

God passed on his handiwork as early as the seventh day, but I notice He has since been rather noncommittal about its merits. I gather either that He spoke too soon, or that trees stand more looking upon than do fig leaves and firmaments.

❀   ❀   ❀

WHY IS THE SHOVEL REGARDED as a symbol of drudgery? Perhaps because most shovels are dull. Certainly all drudges have dull shovels, but I am uncertain which of these two facts is cause and which effect. I only know that a good file, vigorously wielded, makes my shovel sing as it slices the mellow loam. I am told there is music in the sharp plane, the sharp chisel, and the sharp scalpel, but I hear it best in my shovel; it hums in my wrists as I plant a pine. I suspect that the fellow who tried so hard to strike one clear note upon the harp of time chose too difficult an instrument.

It is well that the planting season comes only in spring, for moderation is best in all things, even shovels. During the other months you may watch the process of becoming a pine.

The pine's new year begins in May, when the terminal bud becomes "the candle." Whoever coined that name for the new growth had subtlety in his soul. "The candle" sounds like a platitudinous reference to obvious facts: the new shoot is waxy, upright, brittle. But he who lives with pines knows that candle has a deeper meaning, for at its tip burns the eternal flame that lights a path into the future. May after May my pines follow their candles skyward, each headed straight for the zenith, and each meaning to get there if only there be years enough before the last trumpet blows. It is a very old pine who at last forgets which of his many candles is the most important, and thus flattens his crown against the sky. You may forget, but no pine of your own planting will do so in your lifetime.

Winter pines

If you are thriftily inclined, you will find pines congenial company, for, unlike the hand-to-mouth hardwoods, they never pay current bills out of current earnings; they live solely on their savings of the year before. In fact every pine carries an open bank-book, in which his cash balance is recorded by 30 June of each year. If, on that date, his completed candle has developed a terminal cluster of ten or twelve buds, it means that he has salted away enough rain and sun for a two-foot or even a three-foot thrust skyward next spring. If there are only four or six buds, his thrust will be a lesser one, but he will nevertheless wear that peculiar air that goes with solvency.

Hard years, of course, come to pines as they do to men, and these are recorded as shorter thrusts, i.e. shorter spaces between the successive whorls of branches. These spaces, then, are an autobiography that he who walks with trees may read at will. In order to date a hard year correctly, you must always subtract one from the year of lesser growth. Thus the 1937 growth was short in all pines; this records the universal drouth of 1936. On the other hand the 1941 growth was long in all pines; perhaps they saw the shadow of things to come, and made a special effort to show the world that pines still know where they are going, even though men do not.

When one pine shows a short year but his neighbors do not, you may safely interpolate some purely local or individual adversity: a fire scar, a gnawing meadowmouse, a windburn, or some local bottleneck in that dark laboratory we call the soil.

❧ ❧ ❧

THERE IS MUCH SMALL-TALK and neighborhood gossip among pines. By paying heed to this chatter, I learn what has transpired during the week when I am absent in town. Thus in March, when the deer frequently browse white pines, the height of the browsings tells me how hungry they are. A deer full of corn is too lazy to nip branches more than four feet above the ground; a really hungry deer rises on his hind legs and nips as high as eight feet. Thus I learn the gastronomic status of the deer without seeing them, and I learn, without visiting his field, whether my neighbor has hauled in his cornshocks.

In May, when the new candle is tender and brittle as an asparagus shoot, a bird alighting on it will often break it off. Every spring I find a few such decapitated trees, each with its wilted candle lying in the grass. It is easy to infer what has happened, but in a decade of watching I have never once *seen* a bird break a candle. It is an object lesson: one need not doubt the unseen.

In June of each year a few white pines suddenly show wilted candles, which shortly thereafter turn brown and die. A pine weevil has bored into the terminal bud cluster and deposited eggs; the grubs, when hatched, bore down along the pith and kill the shoot. Such a leaderless pine is doomed to frustration, for the surviving branches disagree among themselves who is to head the skyward march. They all do, and as a consequence the tree remains a bush.

It is a curious circumstance that only pines in full sunlight are bitten by weevils; shaded pines are ignored. Such are the hidden uses of adversity.

In October my pines tell me, by their rubbed-off bark, when the bucks are beginning to "feel their oats." A jackpine about eight feet high, and standing alone, seems especially to incite in a buck the idea that the world needs prodding. Such a tree must perforce turn the other cheek also, and emerges much the worse for wear. The only element of justice in such combats is that the more the tree is punished, the more pitch the buck carries away on his not-so-shiny antlers.

The chit-chat of the woods is sometimes hard to translate. Once in midwinter I found in the droppings under a grouse roost some half-digested structures that I could not identify. They resembled miniature corncobs about half an inch long. I examined samples of every local grouse food I could think of, but without finding any clue to the origin of the "cobs." Finally I cut open the terminal bud of a jackpine, and in its core I found the answer. The grouse had eaten the buds, digested the pitch, rubbed off the scales in his gizzard, and left the cob, which was, in effect, the forthcoming candle. One might say that this grouse had been speculating in jackpine "futures."

      ❧   ❧   ❧

THE THREE SPECIES OF PINE NATIVE TO WISCONSIN (white, red, and jack) differ radically in their opinions about marriageable age. The precocious jackpine sometimes blooms and bears cones a year or two after leaving the nursery, and a few of my 13-year-old jacks already boast of grandchildren. My 13-year-old reds first bloomed this year, but my whites have not yet bloomed; they adhere closely to the Anglo-Saxon doctrine of free, white, and twenty-one.

Were it not for this wide diversity in social outlook, my red squirrels would be much curtailed in their bill-of-fare. Each year in midsummer they start tearing up jackpine cones for the seeds, and no Labor-Day picnic ever scattered more hulls and rinds over the landscape than they do: under each tree the remains of their annual feast lie in piles and heaps. Yet there are always cones to spare, as attested by their progeny popping up among the goldenrods.

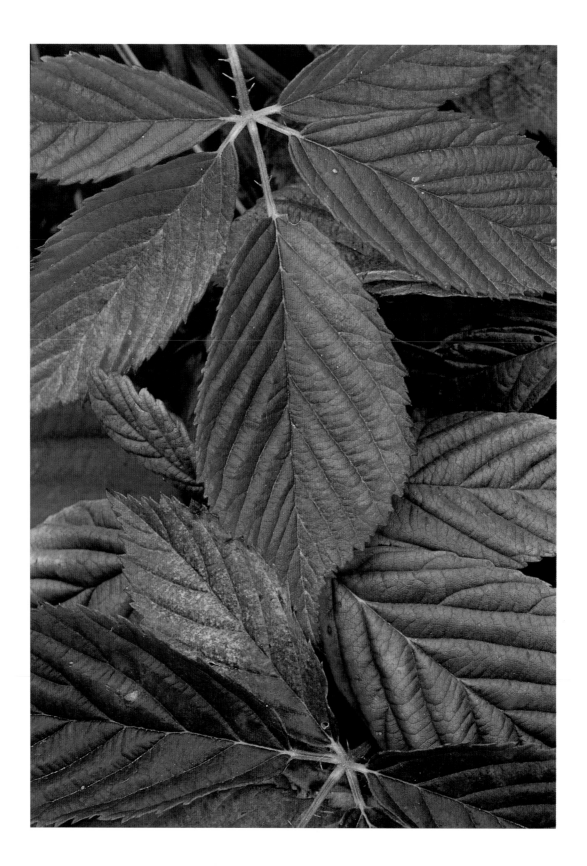

Few people know that pines bear flowers, and most of those who do are too prosy to see in this festival of bloom anything more than a routine biological function. All disillusioned folk should spend the second week in May in a pine woods, and such as wear glasses should take along an extra handkerchief. The prodigality of pine pollen should convince anyone of the reckless exuberance of the season, even when the song of the kinglet has failed to do so.

Young white pines usually thrive best in the absence of their parents. I know of whole woodlots in which the younger generation, even when provided with a place in the sun, is dwarfed and spindled by its elders. Again there are woodlots in which no such inhibition obtains. I wish I knew whether such differences lie in tolerance in the young, in the old, or in the soil.

Pines, like people, are choosy about their associates and do not succeed in suppressing their likes and dislikes. Thus there is an affinity between white pines and dewberries, between red pines and flowering spurge, between jackpines and sweet fern. When I plant a white pine in a dewberry patch, I can safely predict that within a year he will develop a husky cluster of buds, and that his new needles will show that bluish bloom which bespeaks health and congenial company. He will outgrow and outbloom his fellows planted on the same day, with the same care, in the same soil, but in the company of grass.

In October I like to walk among these blue plumes, rising straight and stalwart from the red carpet of dewberry leaves. I wonder whether they are aware of their state of well-being. I know only that I am.

Dewberry leaves

Following pages: pine forest in winter

Pines have earned the reputation of being "evergreen" by the same device that governments use to achieve the appearance of perpetuity: overlapping terms of office. By taking on new needles on the new growth of each year, and discarding old needles at longer intervals, they have led the casual onlooker to believe that needles remain forever green.

Each species of pine has its own constitution, which prescribes a term of office for needles appropriate to its way of life. Thus the white pine retains its needles for a year and a half; the red and jackpines for two years and a half. Incoming needles take office in June, and outgoing needles write farewell addresses in October. All write the same thing, in the same tawny yellow ink, which by November turns brown. Then the needles fall, and are filed in the duff to enrich the wisdom of the stand. It is this accumulated wisdom that hushes the footsteps of whoever walks under pines.

It is in midwinter that I sometimes glean from my pines something more important than woodlot politics, and the news of the wind and weather. This is especially likely to happen on some gloomy evening when the snow has buried all irrelevant detail, and the hush of elemental sadness lies heavy upon every living thing. Nevertheless, my pines, each with his burden of snow, are standing ramrod-straight, rank upon rank, and in the dusk beyond I sense the presence of hundreds more. At such times I feel a curious transfusion of courage.

Pines in winter

65290

TO BAND A BIRD is to hold a ticket in a great lottery. Most of us hold tickets on our own survival, but we buy them from the insurance company, which knows too much to sell us a really sporting chance. It is an exercise in objectivity to hold a ticket on the banded sparrow that falleth, or on the banded chickadee that may some day re-enter your trap, and thus prove that he is still alive.

The tyro gets his thrill from banding new birds; he plays a kind of game against himself, striving to break his previous score for total numbers. But to the old-timer the banding of new birds becomes merely pleasant routine; the real thrill lies in the recapture of some bird banded long ago, some bird whose age, adventures, and previous condition of appetite are perhaps better known to you than to the bird himself.

Thus in our family, the question whether chickadee 65290 would survive for still another winter was, for five years, a sporting question of the first magnitude.

Beginning a decade ago, we have trapped and banded most of the chickadees on our farm each winter. In early winter, the traps yield mostly unbanded birds; these presumably are mostly the young of the year, which, once banded, can thereafter be 'dated.' As the winter wears on, unbanded birds cease to appear in the trap; we then know that the local population consists largely of marked birds. We can tell from the band numbers how many birds are present, and how many of these are survivors from each previous year of banding.

65290 was one of 7 chickadees constituting the "class of 1937." When he first entered our trap, he showed no visible evidence of genius. Like his classmates, his valor for suet was greater than his discretion. Like his classmates, he bit my finger while being taken out of the trap. When banded and released he fluttered up to a limb, pecked his new aluminum anklet in mild annoyance, shook his mussed feathers, cursed gently, and hurried away to catch up with the gang. It is doubtful whether he drew any philosophical deductions from his experience (such as "all is not ants' eggs that glitters"), for he was caught again three times that same winter.

By the second winter our recaptures showed that the class of 7 had shrunk to 3, and by the third winter to 2. By the fifth winter 65290 was the sole survivor of his generation. Signs of genius were still lacking, but of his extraordinary capacity for living, there was now historical proof.

Bird bands and chickadee notes

During his sixth winter 65290 failed to reappear, and the verdict of "missing in action" is now confirmed by his absence during four subsequent trappings.

At that, of 97 chicks banded during the decade, 65290 was the only one contriving to survive for five winters. Three reached 4 years, 7 reached 3 years, 19 reached 2 years, and 67 disappeared after their first winter. Hence if I were selling insurance to chicks, I could compute the premium with assurance. But this would raise the problem: in what currency would I pay the widows? I suppose in ants' eggs.

I know so little about birds that I can only speculate on why 65290 survived his fellows. Was he more clever in dodging his enemies? What enemies? A chickadee is almost too small to have any. That whimsical fellow called Evolution, having enlarged the dinosaur until he tripped over his own toes, tried shrinking the chickadee until he was just too big to be snapped up by flycatchers as an insect, and just too little to be pursued by hawks and owls as meat. Then he regarded his handiwork and laughed. Everyone laughs at so small a bundle of large enthusiasms.

The sparrow hawk, the screech owl, the shrike, and especially the midget saw-whet owl might find it worth while to kill a chickadee, but I've only once found evidence of actual murder: a screech-owl pellet contained one of my bands. Perhaps these small bandits have a fellow-feeling for midgets.

It seems likely that weather is the only killer so devoid of both humor and dimension as to kill a chickadee. I suspect that in the chickadee Sunday School two mortal sins are taught: thou shalt not venture into windy places in winter, thou shalt not get wet before a blizzard.

I learned the second commandment one drizzly winter dusk while watching a band of chicks going to roost in my woods. The drizzle came out of the south, but I could tell it would turn northwest and bitter cold before morning. The chicks went to bed in a dead oak, the bark of which had peeled and warped into curls, cups, and hollows of various sizes, shapes, and exposures. The bird selecting a roost dry against a south drizzle, but vulnerable to a north one, would surely be frozen by morning. The bird selecting a roost dry from all sides would awaken safe. This, I think, is the kind of wisdom that spells survival in chickdom, and accounts for 65290 and his like.

Prairie grass, the Shack meadow

The chickadee's fear of windy places is easily deduced from his behavior. In winter he ventures away from woods only on calm days, and the distance varies inversely as the breeze. I know several wind-swept woodlots that are chickless all winter, but are freely used at all other seasons. They are wind-swept because cows have browsed out the undergrowth. To the steam-heated banker who mortgages the farmer who needs more cows who need more pasture, wind is a minor nuisance, except perhaps at the Flatiron corner. To the chickadee, winter wind is the boundary of the habitable world. If the chickadee had an office, the maxim over his desk would say: "Keep calm."

His behavior at the trap discloses the reason. Turn your trap so that he must enter with even a moderate wind at his tail, and all the king's horses cannot drag him to the bait. Turn it the other way, and your score may be good. Wind from behind blows cold and wet under the feathers, which are his portable roof and air-conditioner. Nuthatches, juncos, tree sparrows, and woodpeckers likewise fear winds from behind, but their heating plants and hence their wind tolerance are larger in the order named. Books on nature seldom mention wind; they are written behind stoves.

I suspect there is a third commandment in chickdom: thou shalt investigate every loud noise. When we start chopping in our woods, the chicks at once appear and stay until the felled tree or roven log has exposed new insect eggs or pupae for their delectation. The discharge of a gun will likewise summon chicks, but with less satisfactory dividends.

What served as their dinner bell before the day of axes, mauls, and guns? Presumably the crash of falling trees. In December 1940, an ice-storm felled an extraordinary number of dead snags and living limbs in our woods. Our chicks scoffed at the trap for a month, being replete with the dividends of the storm.

65290 has long since gone to his reward. I hope that in his new woods, great oaks full of ants' eggs keep falling all day long, with never a wind to ruffle his composure or take the edge off his appetite. And I hope that he still wears my band.

December chickadee

Marshland Elegy

A DAWN WIND STIRS on the great marsh. With almost imperceptible slowness it rolls a bank of fog across the wide morass. Like the white ghost of a glacier the mists advance, riding over phalanxes of tamarack, sliding across bogmeadows heavy with dew. A single silence hangs from horizon to horizon.

Out of some far recess of the sky a tinkling of little bells falls soft upon the listening land. Then again silence. Now comes a baying of some sweet-throated hound, soon the clamor of a responding pack. Then a far clear blast of hunting horns, out of the sky into the fog.

High horns, low horns, silence, and finally a pandemonium of trumpets, rattles, croaks, and cries that almost shakes the bog with its nearness, but without yet disclosing whence it comes. At last a glint of sun reveals the approach of a great echelon of birds. On motionless wing they emerge from the lifting mists, sweep a final arc of sky, and settle in clangorous descending spirals to their feeding grounds. A new day has begun on the crane marsh.

Sandhill cranes landing, the Great Marsh

A SENSE OF TIME LIES THICK AND HEAVY on such a place. Yearly since the ice age it has awakened each spring to the clangor of cranes. The peat layers that comprise the bog are laid down in the basin of an ancient lake. The cranes stand, as it were, upon the sodden pages of their own history. These peats are the compressed remains of the mosses that clogged the pools, of the tamaracks that spread over the moss, of the cranes that bugled over the tamaracks since the retreat of the ice sheet. An endless caravan of generations has built of its own bones this bridge into the future, this habitat where the oncoming host again may live and breed and die.

To what end? Out on the bog a crane, gulping some luckless frog, springs his ungainly hulk into the air and flails the morning sun with mighty wings. The tamaracks re-echo with his bugled certitude. He seems to know.

❦   ❦   ❦

OUR ABILITY TO PERCEIVE QUALITY IN NATURE BEGINS, as in art, with the pretty. It expands through successive stages of the beautiful to values as yet uncaptured by language. The quality of cranes lies, I think, in this higher gamut, as yet beyond the reach of words.

This much, though, can be said: our appreciation of the crane grows with the slow unraveling of earthly history. His tribe, we now know, stems out of the remote Eocene. The other members of the fauna in which he originated are long since entombed within the hills. When we hear his call we hear no mere bird. We hear the trumpet in the orchestra of evolution. He is the symbol of our untamable past, of that incredible sweep of millennia which underlies and conditions the daily affairs of birds and men.

And so they live and have their being—these cranes—not in the constricted present, but in the wider reaches of evolutionary time. Their annual return is the ticking of the geologic clock. Upon the place of their return they confer a peculiar distinction. Amid the endless mediocrity of the commonplace, a crane marsh holds a paleontological patent of nobility, won in the march of aeons, and revocable only by shotgun. The sadness discernible in some marshes arises, perhaps, from their once having harbored cranes. Now they stand humbled, adrift in history.

Some sense of this quality in cranes seems to have been felt by sportsmen and ornithologists of all ages. Upon such quarry as this the Holy Roman Emperor Frederick loosed his gyrfalcons. Upon such quarry as this once swooped the hawks of Kublai Khan. Marco Polo tells us: "He derives the highest amusement from sporting with gyrfalcons and hawks. At Changanor the Khan has a great Palace surrounded by a fine plain where are found cranes in great numbers. He causes millet and other grains to be sown in order that the birds may not want."

Sandhill cranes

The ornithologist Bengt Berg, seeing cranes as a boy upon the Swedish heaths, forthwith made them his life work. He followed them to Africa and discovered their winter retreat on the White Nile. He says of his first encounter: "It was a spectacle which eclipsed the flight of the roc in the Thousand and One Nights."

⚜   ⚜   ⚜

WHEN THE GLACIER CAME DOWN OUT OF THE NORTH, crunching hills and gouging valleys, some adventuring rampart of the ice climbed the Baraboo Hills and fell back into the outlet gorge of the Wisconsin River. The swollen waters backed up and formed a lake half as long as the state, bordered on the east by cliffs of ice, and fed by the torrents that fell from melting mountains. The shorelines of this old lake are still visible; its bottom is the bottom of the great marsh.

The lake rose through the centuries, finally spilling over east of the Baraboo range. There it cut a new channel for the river, and thus drained itself. To the residual lagoons came the cranes, bugling the defeat of the retreating winter, summoning the on-creeping host of living things to their collective task of marsh-building. Floating bogs of sphagnum moss clogged the lowered waters, filled them. Sedge and leatherleaf, tamarack and spruce successively advanced over the bog, anchoring it by their root fabric, sucking out its water, making peat. The lagoons disappeared, but not the cranes. To the moss-meadows that replaced the ancient waterways they returned each spring to dance and bugle and rear their gangling sorrel-colored young. These, albeit birds, are not properly called chicks, but *colts*. I cannot explain why. On some dewy June morning watch them gambol over their ancestral pastures at the heels of the roan mare, and you will see for yourself.

One year not long ago a French trapper in buckskins pushed his canoe up one of the moss-clogged creeks that thread the great marsh. At this attempt to invade their miry stronghold the cranes gave vent to loud and ribald laughter. A century or two later Englishmen came in covered wagons. They chopped clearings in the timbered moraines that border the marsh, and in them planted corn and buckwheat. They did not intend, like the Great Khan at Changanor, to feed the cranes. But the cranes do not question the intent of glaciers, emperors, or pioneers. They ate the grain, and when some irate farmer failed to concede their usufruct in his corn, they trumpeted a warning and sailed across the marsh to another farm.

There was no alfalfa in those days, and the hill-farms made poor hay land, especially in dry years. One dry year someone set a fire in the tamaracks. The burn grew up quickly to bluejoint grass, which, when cleared of dead trees, made a dependable hay meadow. After that, each August, men appeared to cut hay. In winter, after the cranes had gone South, they drove wagons over the frozen bogs and hauled the hay to their farms in the hills. Yearly they plied the marsh with fire and axe, and in two short decades hay meadows dotted the whole expanse.

Each August when the haymakers came to pitch their camps, singing and drinking and lashing their teams with whip and tongue, the cranes whinnied to their colts and retreated to the far fastnesses. "Red shitepokes" the haymakers called them, from the rusty hue which at that season often stains the battleship-gray of crane plumage. After the hay was stacked and the marsh again their own, the cranes returned, to call down out of October skies the migrant flocks from Canada. Together they wheeled over the new-cut stubbles and raided the corn until frosts gave the signal for the winter exodus.

These haymeadow days were the Arcadian age for marsh dwellers. Man and beast, plant and soil lived on and with each other in mutual toleration, to the mutual benefit of all. The marsh might have kept on producing hay and prairie chickens, deer and muskrat, crane-music and cranberries forever.

The new overlords did not understand this. They did not include soil, plants, or birds in their ideas of mutuality. The dividends of such a balanced economy were too modest. They envisaged farms not only around, but *in* the marsh. An epidemic of ditch-digging and land-booming set in. The marsh was gridironed with drainage canals, speckled with new fields and farmsteads.

But crops were poor and beset by frosts, to which the expensive ditches added an aftermath of debt. Farmers moved out. Peat beds dried, shrank, caught fire. Sun-energy out of the Pleistocene shrouded the countryside in acrid smoke. No man raised his voice against the waste, only his nose against the smell. After a dry summer not even the winter snows could extinguish the smoldering marsh. Great pockmarks were burned into field and meadow, the scars reaching down to the sands of the old lake, peat-covered these hundred centuries. Rank weeds sprang out of the ashes, to be followed after a year or two by aspen scrub. The cranes were hard put, their numbers shrinking with the remnants of unburned meadow. For them, the song of the power shovel came near being an elegy. The high priests of progress knew nothing of cranes, and cared less. What is a species more or less among engineers? What good is an undrained marsh anyhow?

For a decade or two crops grew poorer, fires deeper, wood-fields larger, and cranes scarcer, year by year. Only reflooding, it appeared, could keep the peat from burning. Meanwhile cranberry growers had, by plugging drainage ditches, reflooded a few spots and obtained good yields. Distant politicians bugled about marginal land, over-production, unemployment relief, conservation. Economists and planners came to look at the marsh. Surveyors, technicians, CCC's, buzzed about. A counter-epidemic of reflooding set in. Government bought land, resettled farmers, plugged ditches whole-sale. Slowly the bogs are re-wetting. The firepocks become ponds. Grass fires still burn, but they can no longer burn the wetted soil.

All this, once the CCC camps were gone, was good for cranes, but not so the thickets of scrub popple that spread inexorably over the old burns, and still less the maze of new roads that inevitably follow governmental conservation. To build a road is so much simpler than to think of what the country really needs. A roadless marsh is seemingly as worthless to the alphabetical conservationist as an undrained one was to the empire-builders. Solitude, the one natural resource still undowered of alphabets, is so far recognized as valuable only by ornithologists and cranes.

Thus always does history, whether of marsh or market place, end in paradox. The ultimate value in these marshes is wildness, and the crane is wildness incarnate. But all conservation of wildness is self-defeating, for to cherish we must see and fondle, and when enough have seen and fondled, there is no wilderness left to cherish.

꿍   꿍   꿍

SOME DAY, perhaps in the very process of our benefactions, perhaps in the fullness of geologic time, the last crane will trumpet his farewell and spiral skyward from the great marsh. High out of the clouds will fall the sound of hunting horns, the baying of the phantom pack, the tinkle of little bells, and then a silence never to be broken, unless perchance in some far pasture of the Milky Way.

Sandhill cranes

The Land Ethic

WHEN GOD-LIKE ODYSSEUS RETURNED FROM THE WARS IN TROY, he hanged all on one rope a dozen slave-girls of his household whom he suspected of misbehavior during his absence.

This hanging involved no question of propriety. The girls were property. The disposal of property was then, as now, a matter of expediency, not of right and wrong.

Concepts of right and wrong were not lacking from Odysseus' Greece: witness the fidelity of his wife through the long years before at last his black-prowed galleys clove the wine-dark seas for home. The ethical structure of that day covered wives, but had not yet been extended to human chattels. During the three thousand years which have since elapsed, ethical criteria have been extended to many fields of conduct, with corresponding shrinkages in those judged by expediency only.

Red fox near Alder Creek

The Ethical Sequence

THIS EXTENSION OF ETHICS, so far studied only by philosophers, is actually a process in ecological evolution. Its sequences may be described in ecological as well as in philosophical terms. An ethic, ecologically, is a limitation on freedom of action in the struggle for existence. An ethic, philosophically, is a differentiation of social from anti-social conduct. These are two definitions of one thing. The thing has its origin in the tendency of interdependent individuals or groups to evolve modes of cooperation. The ecologist calls these symbioses. Politics and economics are advanced symbioses in which the original free-for-all competition has been replaced, in part, by co-operative mechanisms with an ethical content.

The complexity of co-operative mechanisms has increased with population density, and with the efficiency of tools. It was simpler, for example, to define the anti-social uses of sticks and stones in the days of the mastodons than of bullets and billboards in the age of motors.

The first ethics dealt with the relation between individuals; the Mosaic Decalogue is an example. Later accretions dealt with the relation between the individual and society. The Golden Rule tries to integrate the individual to society; democracy to integrate social organization to the individual.

There is as yet no ethic dealing with man's relation to land and to the animals and plants which grow upon it. Land, like Odysseus' slave-girls, is still property. The land-relation is still strictly economic, entailing privileges but not obligations.

The extension of ethics to this third element in human environment is, if I read the evidence correctly, an evolutionary possibility and an ecological necessity. It is the third step in a sequence. The first two have already been taken. Individual thinkers since the days of Ezekiel and Isaiah have asserted that the despoliation of land is not only inexpedient but wrong. Society, however, has not yet affirmed their belief. I regard the present conservation movement as the embryo of such an affirmation.

An ethic may be regarded as a mode of guidance for meeting ecological situations so new or intricate, or involving such deferred reactions, that the path of social expediency is not discernible to the average individual. Animal instincts are modes of guidance for the individual in meeting such situations. Ethics are possibly a kind of community instinct in-the-making.

Trillium in bloom

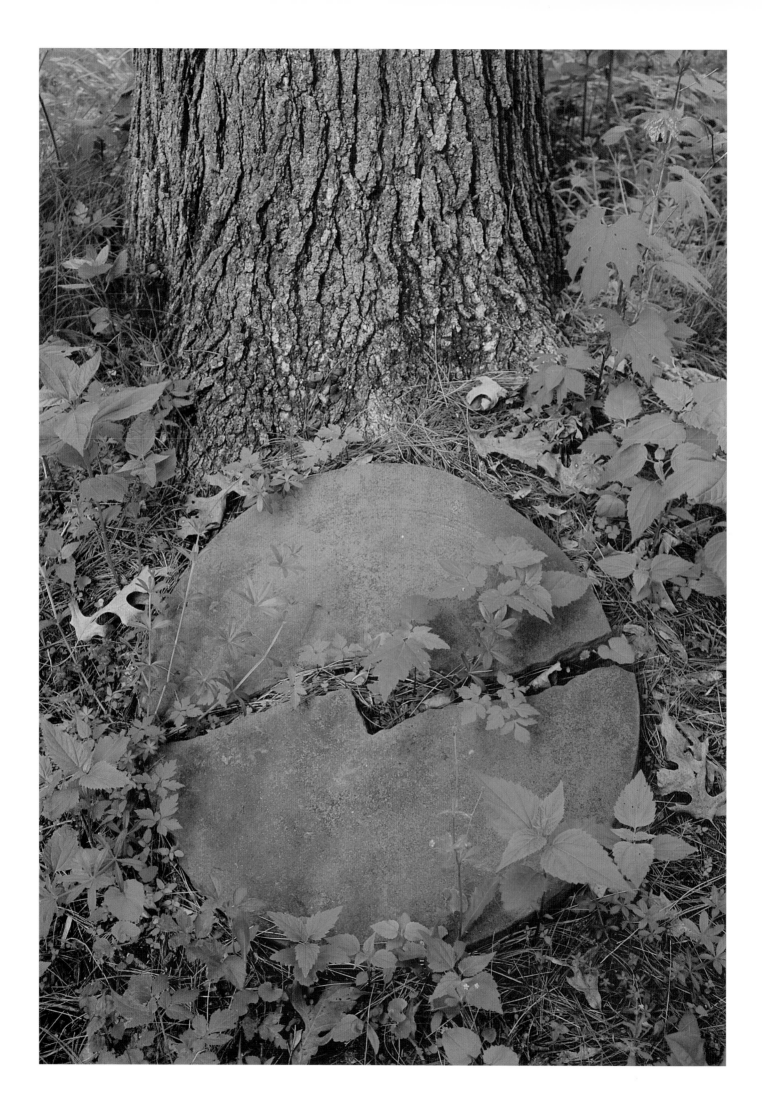

The Community Concept

ALL ETHICS SO FAR EVOLVED REST UPON A SINGLE PREMISE: that the individual is a member of a community of interdependent parts. His instincts prompt him to compete for his place in that community, but his ethics prompt him also to co-operate (perhaps in order that there may be a place to compete for).

The land ethic simply enlarges the boundaries of the community to include soils, waters, plants, and animals, or collectively: the land.

This sounds simple: do we not already sing our love for and obligation to the land of the free and the home of the brave? Yes, but just what and whom do we love? Certainly not the soil, which we are sending helter-skelter downriver. Certainly not the waters, which we assume have no function except to turn turbines, float barges, and carry off sewage. Certainly not the plants, of which we exterminate whole communities without batting an eye. Certainly not the animals, of which we have already extirpated many of the largest and most beautiful species. A land ethic of course cannot prevent the alteration, management, and use of these "resources," but it does affirm their right to continued existence, and, at least in spots, their continued existence in a natural state.

In short, a land ethic changes the role of *Homo sapiens* from conqueror of the land-community to plain member and citizen of it. It implies respect for his fellow-members, and also respect for the community as such.

In human history, we have learned (I hope) that the conqueror role is eventually self-defeating. Why? Because it is implicit in such a role that the conqueror knows, *ex cathedra*, just what makes the community clock tick, and just what and who is valuable, and what and who is worthless, in community life. It always turns out that he knows neither, and this is why his conquests eventually defeat themselves.

In the biotic community, a parallel situation exists. Abraham knew exactly what the land was for: it was to drip milk and honey into Abraham's mouth. At the present moment, the assurance with which we regard this assumption is inverse to the degree of our education.

The ordinary citizen today assumes that science knows what makes the community clock tick; the scientist is equally sure that he does not. He knows that the biotic mechanism is so complex that its workings may never be fully understood.

That man is, in fact, only a member of a biotic team is shown by an ecological interpretation of history. Many historical events, hitherto explained solely in terms of human enterprise, were actually biotic interactions between people and land. The characteristics of the land determined the facts quite as potently as the characteristics of the men who lived on it.

Aldo's axe-grinding wheel in spring

Consider, for example, the settlement of the Mississippi valley. In the years following the Revolution, three groups were contending for its control: the native Indian, the French and English traders, and the American settlers. Historians wonder what would have happened if the English at Detroit had thrown a little more weight into the Indian side of those tipsy scales which decided the outcome of the colonial migration into the cane-lands of Kentucky. It is time now to ponder the fact that the cane-lands, when subjected to the particular mixture of forces represented by the cow, plow, fire, and axe of the pioneer, became bluegrass. What if the plant succession inherent in this dark and bloody ground had, under the impact of these forces, given us some worthless sedge, shrub, or weed? Would Boone and Kenton have held out? Would there have been any overflow into Ohio, Indiana, Illinois, and Missouri? Any Louisiana Purchase? Any transcontinental union of new states? Any Civil War?

Kentucky was one sentence in the drama of history. We are commonly told what the human actors in this drama tried to do, but we are seldom told that their success, or the lack of it, hung in large degree on the reaction of particular soils to the impact of the particular forces exerted by their occupancy. In the case of Kentucky, we do not even know where the bluegrass came from—whether it is a native species, or a stowaway from Europe.

Contrast the cane-lands with what hindsight tells us about the Southwest, where the pioneers were equally brave, resourceful, and persevering. The impact of occupancy here brought no bluegrass, or other plant fitted to withstand the bumps and buffetings of hard use. This region, when grazed by livestock, reverted through a series of more and more worthless grasses, shrubs, and weeds to a condition of unstable equilibrium. Each recession of plant types bred erosion; each increment to erosion bred a further recession of plants. The result today is a progressive and mutual deterioration, not only of plants and soils, but of the animal community subsisting thereon. The early settlers did not expect this: on the ciénegas of New Mexico some even cut ditches to hasten it. So subtle has been its progress that few residents of the region are aware of it. It is quite invisible to the tourist who finds this wrecked landscape colorful and charming (as indeed it is, but it bears scant resemblance to what it was in 1848).

This same landscape was "developed" once before, but with quite different results. The Pueblo Indians settled the Southwest in pre-Columbian times, but they happened *not* to be equipped with range livestock. Their civilization expired, but not because their land expired.

In India, regions devoid of any sod-forming grass have been settled, apparently without wrecking the land, by the simple expedient of carrying the grass to the cow, rather than vice versa. (Was this the result of some deep wisdom, or was it just good luck? I do not know.)

In short, the plant succession steered the course of history; the pioneer simply demonstrated, for good or ill, what successions inhered in the land. Is history taught in this spirit? It will be, once the concept of land as a community really penetrates our intellectual life.

The Ecological Conscience

CONSERVATION IS A STATE OF HARMONY between men and land. Despite nearly a century of propaganda, conservation still proceeds at a snail's pace; progress still consists largely of letterhead pieties and convention oratory. On the back forty we still slip two steps backward for each forward stride.

The usual answer to this dilemma is "more conservation education." No one will debate this, but is it certain that only the *volume* of education needs stepping up? Is something lacking in the *content* as well?

It is difficult to give a fair summary of its content in brief form, but, as I understand it, the content is substantially this: obey the law, vote right, join some organizations, and practice what conservation is profitable on your own land; the government will do the rest.

Is not this formula too easy to accomplish anything worth-while? It defines no right or wrong, assigns no obligation, calls for no sacrifice, implies no change in the current philosophy of values. In respect of land-use, it urges only enlightened self-interest. Just how far will such education take us? An example will perhaps yield a partial answer.

By 1930 it had become clear to all except the ecologically blind that southwestern Wisconsin's topsoil was slipping seaward. In 1933 the farmers were told that if they would adopt certain remedial practices for five years, the public would donate CCC labor to install them, plus the necessary machinery and materials. The offer was widely accepted, but the practices were widely forgotten when the five-year contract period was up. The farmers continued only those practices that yielded an immediate and visible economic gain for themselves.

This led to the idea that maybe farmers would learn more quickly if they themselves wrote the rules. Accordingly the Wisconsin Legislature in 1937 passed the Soil Conservation District Law. This said to farmers, in effect: *We, the public, will furnish you free technical service and loan you specialized machinery, if you will write your own rules for land-use. Each county may write its own rules, and these will have the force of law.* Nearly all the counties promptly organized to accept the proffered help, but after a decade of operation, *no county has yet written a single rule.* There has been visible progress in such practices as strip-cropping, pasture renovation, and soil liming, but none in fencing woodlots against grazing, and none in excluding plow and cow from steep slopes. The farmers, in short, have selected those remedial practices which were profitable anyhow, and ignored those which were profitable to the community, but not clearly profitable to themselves.

When one asks why no rules have been written, one is told that the community is not yet ready to support them; education must precede rules. But the education actually in progress makes no mention of obligations to land over and above those dictated by self-interest. The net result is that we have more education but less soil, fewer healthy woods, and as many floods as in 1937.

The puzzling aspect of such situations is that the existence of obligations over and above self-interest is taken for granted in such rural community enterprises as the betterment of roads, schools, churches, and baseball teams. Their existence is not taken for granted, nor as yet seriously discussed, in bettering the behavior of the water that falls on the land, or in the preserving of the beauty or diversity of the farm landscape. Land-use ethics are still governed wholly by economic self-interest, just as social ethics were a century ago.

To sum up: we asked the farmer to do what he conveniently could to save his soil, and he has done just that, and only that. The farmer who clears the woods off a 75 per cent slope, turns his cows into the clearing, and dumps its rainfall, rocks, and soil into the community creek, is still (if otherwise decent) a respected member of society. If he puts lime on his fields and plants his crops on contour, he is still entitled to all the privileges and emoluments of his Soil Conservation District. The District is a beautiful piece of social machinery, but it is coughing along on two cylinders because we have been too timid, and too anxious for quick success, to tell the farmer the true magnitude of his obligations. Obligations have no meaning without conscience, and the problem we face is the extension of the social conscience from people to land.

No important change in ethics was ever accomplished without an internal change in our intellectual emphasis, loyalties, affections, and convictions. The proof that conservation has not yet touched these foundations of conduct lies in the fact that philosophy and religion have not yet heard of it. In our attempt to make conservation easy, we have made it trivial.

Pasque flowers

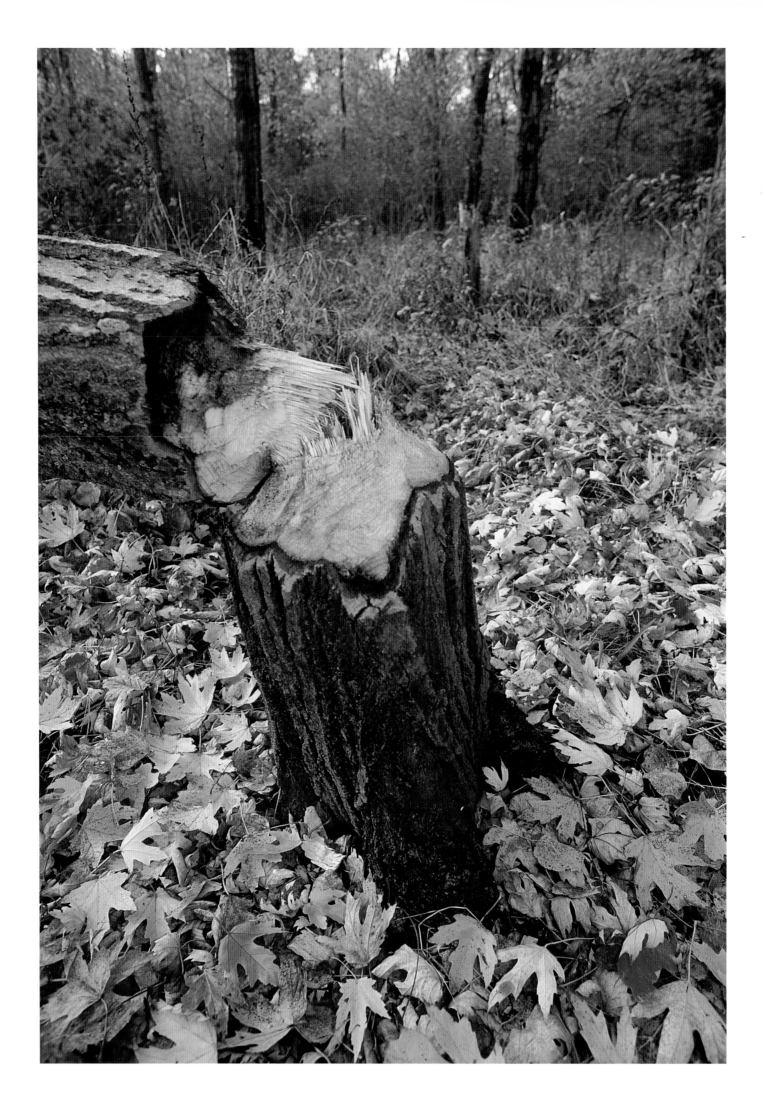

Substitutes for a Land Ethic

WHEN THE LOGIC OF HISTORY HUNGERS FOR BREAD AND WE HAND OUT A STONE, we are at pains to explain how much the stone resembles bread. I now describe some of the stones which serve in lieu of a land ethic.

One basic weakness in a conservation system based wholly on economic motives is that most members of the land community have no economic value. Wildflowers and songbirds are examples. Of the 22,000 higher plants and animals native to Wisconsin, it is doubtful whether more than 5 per cent can be sold, fed, eaten, or otherwise put to economic use. Yet these creatures are members of the biotic community, and if (as I believe) its stability depends on its integrity, they are entitled to continuance.

When one of these non-economic categories is threatened, and if we happen to love it, we invent subterfuges to give it economic importance. At the beginning of the century songbirds were supposed to be disappearing. Ornithologists jumped to the rescue with some distinctly shaky evidence to the effect that insects would eat us up if birds failed to control them. The evidence had to be economic in order to be valid.

It is painful to read these circumlocutions today. We have no land ethic yet, but we have at least drawn nearer the point of admitting that birds should continue as a matter of biotic right, regardless of the presence or absence of economic advantage to us.

A parallel situation exists in respect of predatory mammals, raptorial birds, and fish-eating birds. Time was when biologists somewhat overworked the evidence that these creatures preserve the health of game by killing weaklings, or that they control rodents for the farmer, or that they prey only on "worthless" species. Here again, the evidence had to be economic in order to be valid. It is only in recent years that we hear the more honest argument that predators are members of the community, and that no special interest has the right to exterminate them for the sake of a benefit, real or fancied, to itself. Unfortunately this enlightened view is still in the talk stage. In the field the extermination of predators goes merrily on: witness the impending erasure of the timber wolf by fiat of Congress, the Conservation Bureaus, and many state legislatures.

Beaver-felled maple

Some species of trees have been "read out of the party" by economics-minded foresters because they grow too slowly, or have too low a sale value to pay as timber crops: white cedar, tamarack, cypress, beech, and hemlock are examples. In Europe, where forestry is ecologically more advanced, the non-commercial tree species are recognized as members of the native forest community, to be preserved as such, within reason. Moreover some (like beech) have been found to have a valuable function in building up soil fertility. The interdependence of the forest and its constituent tree species, ground flora, and fauna is taken for granted.

Lack of economic value is sometimes a character not only of species or groups, but of entire biotic communities: marshes, bogs, dunes, and "deserts" are examples. Our formula in such cases is to relegate their conservation to government as refuges, monuments, or parks. The difficulty is that these communities are usually interspersed with more valuable private lands; the government cannot possibly own or control such scattered parcels. The net effect is that we have relegated some of them to ultimate extinction over large areas. If the private owner were ecologically minded, he would be proud to be the custodian of a reasonable proportion of such areas, which add diversity and beauty to his farm and to his community.

In some instances, the assumed lack of profit in these "waste" areas has proved to be wrong, but only after most of them had been done away with. The present scramble to reflood muskrat marshes is a case in point.

There is a clear tendency in American conservation to relegate to government all necessary jobs that private landowners fail to perform. Government ownership, operation, subsidy, or regulation is now widely prevalent in forestry, range management, soil and watershed management, park and wilderness conservation, fisheries management, and migratory bird management, with more to come. Most of this growth in governmental conservation is proper and logical, some of it is inevitable. That I imply no disapproval of it is implicit in the fact that I have spent most of my life working for it. Nevertheless the question arises: What is the ultimate magnitude of the enterprise? Will the tax base carry its eventual ramifications? At what point will governmental conservation, like the mastodon, become handicapped by its own dimensions? The answer, if there is any, seems to be in a land ethic, or some other force which assigns more obligation to the private landowner.

Industrial landowners and users, especially lumbermen and stockmen, are inclined to wail long and loudly about the extension of government ownership and regulation to land, but (with notable exceptions) they show little disposition to develop the only visible alternative: the voluntary practice of conservation on their own lands.

When the private landowner is asked to perform some unprofitable act for the good of the community, he today assents only with outstretched palm. If the act costs him cash this is fair and proper, but when it costs only forethought, open-mindedness, or time, the issue is at least debatable. The overwhelming growth of land-use subsidies in recent years must be ascribed, in large part, to the government's own agencies for conservation education: the land bureaus, the agricultural colleges, and the extension services. As far as I can detect, no ethical obligation toward land is taught in these institutions.

To sum up: a system of conservation based solely on economic self-interest is hopelessly lopsided. It tends to ignore, and thus eventually to eliminate, many elements in the land community that lack commercial value, but that are (as far as we know) essential to its healthy functioning. It assumes, falsely, I think, that the economic parts of the biotic clock will function without the uneconomic parts. It tends to relegate to government many functions eventually too large, too complex, or too widely dispersed to be performed by government.

An ethical obligation on the part of the private owner is the only visible remedy for these situations.

The Land Pyramid

AN ETHIC TO SUPPLEMENT AND GUIDE the economic relation to land presupposes the existence of some mental image of land as a biotic mechanism. We can be ethical only in relation to something we can see, feel, understand, love, or otherwise have faith in.

The image commonly employed in conservation education is "the balance of nature." For reasons too lengthy to detail here, this figure of speech fails to describe accurately what little we know about the land mechanism. A much truer image is the one employed in ecology: the biotic pyramid. I shall first sketch the pyramid as a symbol of land, and later develop some of its implications in terms of land-use.

Plants absorb energy from the sun. This energy flows through a circuit called the biota, which may be represented by a pyramid consisting of layers. The bottom layer is the soil. A plant layer rests on the soil, an insect layer on the plants, a bird and rodent layer on the insects, and so on up through various animal groups to the apex layer, which consists of the larger carnivores.

The species of a layer are alike not in where they came from, or in what they look like, but rather in what they eat. Each successive layer depends on those below it for food and often for other services, and each in turn furnishes food and services to those above. Proceeding upward, each successive layer decreases in numerical abundance. Thus, for every carnivore there are hundreds of his prey, thousands of their prey, millions of insects, uncountable plants. The pyramidal form of the system reflects this numerical progression from apex to base. Man shares an intermediate layer with the bears, raccoons, and squirrels which eat both meat and vegetables.

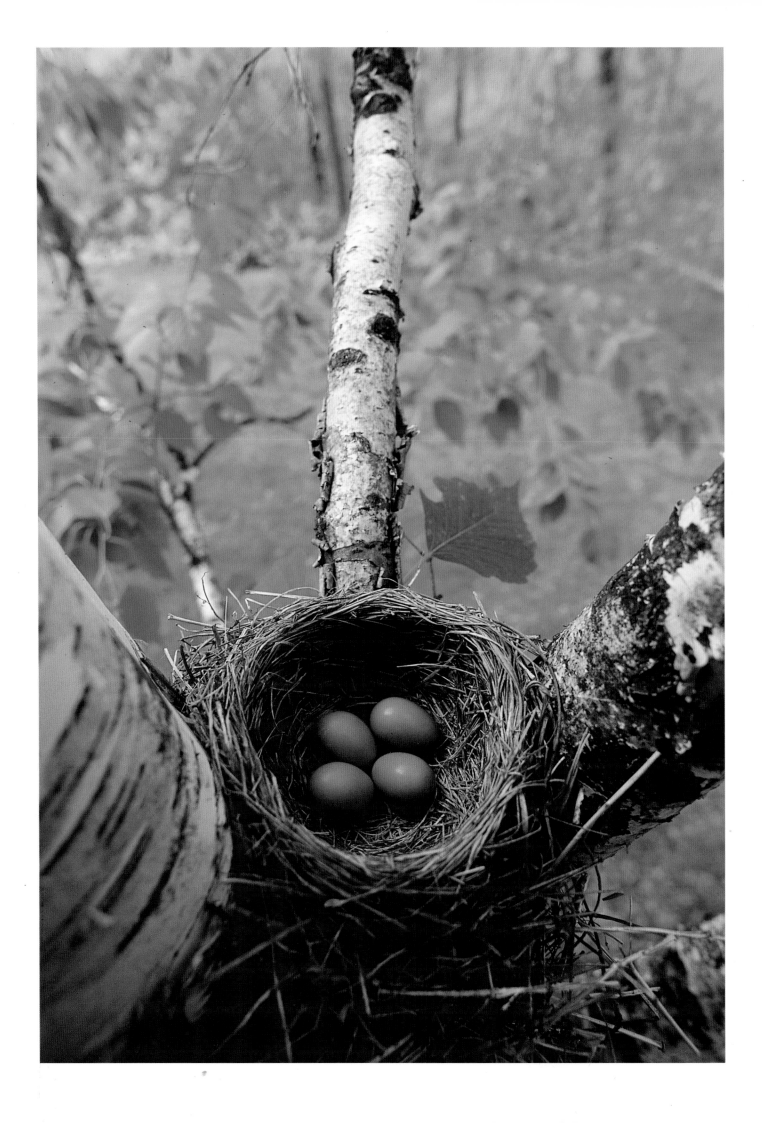

The lines of dependency for food and other services are called food chains. Thus soil-oak-deer-Indian is a chain that has now been largely converted to soil-corn-cow-farmer. Each species, including ourselves, is a link in many chains. The deer eats a hundred plants other than oak, and the cow a hundred plants other than corn. Both, then, are links in a hundred chains. The pyramid is a tangle of chains so complex as to seem disorderly, yet the stability of the system proves it to be a highly organized structure. Its functioning depends on the co-operation and competition of its diverse parts.

In the beginning, the pyramid of life was low and squat; the food chains short and simple. Evolution has added layer after layer, link after link. Man is one of thousands of accretions to the height and complexity of the pyramid. Science has given us many doubts, but it has given us at least one certainty: the trend of evolution is to elaborate and diversify the biota.

Land, then, is not merely soil; it is a fountain of energy flowing through a circuit of soils, plants, and animals. Food chains are the living channels which conduct energy upward; death and decay return it to the soil. The circuit is not closed; some energy is dissipated in decay, some is added by absorption from the air, some is stored in soils, peats, and long-lived forests; but it is a sustained circuit, like a slowly augmented revolving fund of life. There is always a net loss by downhill wash, but this is normally small and offset by the decay of rocks. It is deposited in the ocean and, in the course of geological time, raised to form new lands and new pyramids.

The velocity and character of the upward flow of energy depend on the complex structure of the plant and animal community, much as the upward flow of sap in a tree depends on its complex cellular organization. Without this complexity, normal circulation would presumably not occur. Structure means the characteristic numbers, as well as the characteristic kinds and functions, of the component species. This interdependence between the complex structure of the land and its smooth functioning as an energy unit is one of its basic attributes.

When a change occurs in one part of the circuit, many other parts must adjust themselves to it. Change does not necessarily obstruct or divert the flow of energy; evolution is a long series of self-induced changes, the net result of which has been to elaborate the flow mechanism and to lengthen the circuit. Evolutionary changes, however, are usually slow and local. Man's invention of tools has enabled him to make changes of unprecedented violence, rapidity, and scope.

Robin's nest

One change is in the composition of floras and faunas. The larger predators are lopped off the apex of the pyramid; food chains, for the first time in history, become shorter rather than longer. Domesticated species from other lands are substituted for wild ones, and wild ones are moved to new habitats. In this world-wide pooling of faunas and floras, some species get out of bounds as pests and diseases, others are extinguished. Such effects are seldom intended or foreseen; they represent unpredicted and often untraceable readjustments in the structure. Agricultural science is largely a race between the emergence of new pests and the emergence of new techniques for their control.

Another change touches the flow of energy through plants and animals and its return to the soil. Fertility is the ability of soil to receive, store, and release energy. Agriculture, by overdrafts on the soil, or by too radical a substitution of domestic for native species in the superstructure, may derange the channels of flow or deplete storage. Soils depleted of their storage, or of the organic matter which anchors it, wash away faster than they form. This is erosion.

Waters, like soil, are part of the energy circuit. Industry, by polluting waters or obstructing them with dams, may exclude the plants and animals necessary to keep energy in circulation.

Transportation brings about another basic change: the plants or animals grown in one region are now consumed and returned to the soil in another. Transportation taps the energy stored in rocks, and in the air, and uses it elsewhere; thus we fertilize the garden with nitrogen gleaned by the guano birds from the fishes of seas on the other side of the Equator. Thus the formerly localized and self-contained circuits are pooled on a world-wide scale.

The process of altering the pyramid for human occupation releases stored energy, and this often gives rise, during the pioneering period, to a deceptive exuberance of plant and animal life, both wild and tame. These releases of biotic capital tend to becloud or postpone the penalties of violence.

❧   ❧   ❧

THIS THUMBNAIL SKETCH OF LAND as an energy circuit conveys three basic ideas:

(1)   That land is not merely soil.

(2)   That the native plants and animals kept the energy circuit open; others may or may not.

(3)   That man-made changes are of a different order than evolutionary changes, and have effects more comprehensive than is intended or foreseen.

These ideas, collectively, raise two basic issues: Can the land adjust itself to the new order? Can the desired alterations be accomplished with less violence?

Biotas seem to differ in their capacity to sustain violent conversion. Western Europe, for example, carries a far different pyramid than Caesar found there. Some large animals are lost; swampy forests have become meadows or plow-land; many new plants and animals are introduced, some of which escape as pests; the remaining natives are greatly changed in distribution and abundance. Yet the soil is still there and, with the help of imported nutrients, still fertile; the waters flow normally; the new structure seems to function and to persist. There is no visible stoppage or derangement of the circuit.

Western Europe, then, has a resistant biota. Its inner processes are tough, elastic, resistant to strain. No matter how violent the alterations, the pyramid, so far, has developed some new *modus vivendi* which preserves its habitability for man, and for most of the other natives.

Japan seems to present another instance of radical conversion without disorganization.

Most other civilized regions, and some as yet barely touched by civilization, display various stages of disorganization, varying from initial symptoms to advanced wastage. In Asia Minor and North Africa diagnosis is confused by climatic changes, which may have been either the cause or the effect of advanced wastage. In the United States the degree of disorganization varies locally; it is worst in the Southwest, the Ozarks, and parts of the South, and least in New England and the Northwest. Better land-uses may still arrest it in the less advanced regions. In parts of Mexico, South America, South Africa, and Australia a violent and accelerating wastage is in progress, but I cannot assess the prospects.

This almost world-wide display of disorganization in the land seems to be similar to disease in an animal, except that it never culminates in complete disorganization or death. The land recovers, but at some reduced level of complexity, and with a reduced carrying capacity for people, plants, and animals. Many biotas currently regarded as "lands of opportunity" are in fact already subsisting on exploitative agriculture, i.e. they have already exceeded their sustained carrying capacity. Most of South America is overpopulated in this sense.

In arid regions we attempt to offset the process of wastage by reclamation, but it is only too evident that the prospective longevity of reclamation projects is often short. In our own West, the best of them may not last a century.

The combined evidence of history and ecology seems to support one general deduction: the less violent the manmade changes, the greater the probability of successful readjustment in the pyramid. Violence, in turn, varies with human population density; a dense population requires a more violent conversion. In this respect, North America has a better chance for permanence than Europe, if she can contrive to limit her density.

Following pages: wildflowers, forest floor

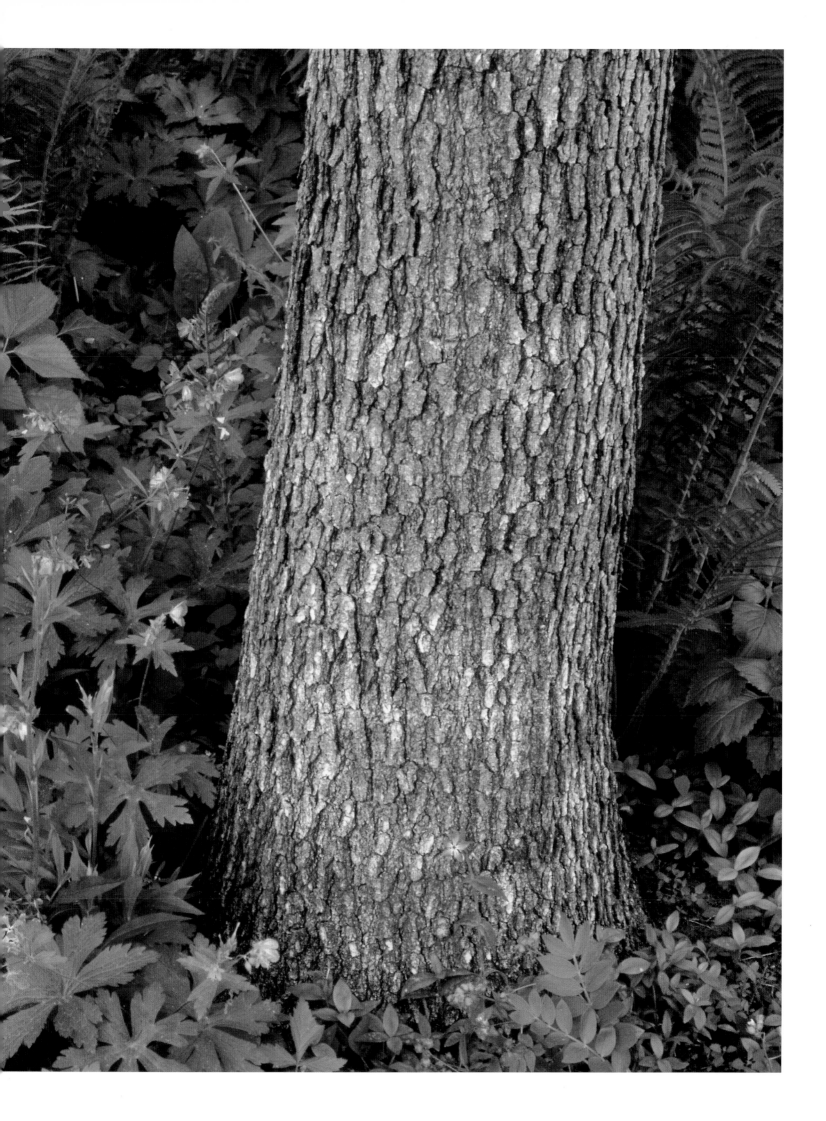

This deduction runs counter to our current philosophy, which assumes that because a small increase in density enriched human life, that an indefinite increase will enrich it indefinitely. Ecology knows of no density relationship that holds for indefinitely wide limits. All gains from density are subject to a law of diminishing returns.

Whatever may be the equation for men and land, it is improbable that we as yet know all its terms. Recent discoveries in mineral and vitamin nutrition reveal unsuspected dependencies in the up-circuit: incredibly minute quantities of certain substances determine the value of soils to plants, of plants to animals. What of the down-circuit? What of the vanishing species, the preservation of which we now regard as an esthetic luxury? They helped build the soil; in what unsuspected ways may they be essential to its maintenance? Professor Weaver proposes that we use prairie flowers to reflocculate the wasting soils of the dust bowl; who knows for what purpose cranes and condors, otters and grizzlies may some day be used?

Land Health and the A-B Cleavage

A LAND ETHIC, then, reflects the existence of an ecological conscience, and this in turn reflects a conviction of individual responsibility for the health of the land. Health is the capacity of the land for self-renewal. Conservation is our effort to understand and preserve this capacity.

Conservationists are notorious for their dissensions. Superficially these seem to add up to mere confusion, but a more careful scrutiny reveals a single plane of cleavage common to many specialized fields. In each field one group (A) regards the land as soil, and its function as commodity-production; another group (B) regards the land as a biota, and its function as something broader. How much broader is admittedly in a state of doubt and confusion.

In my own field, forestry, Group A is quite content to grow trees like cabbages, with cellulose as the basic forest commodity. It feels no inhibition against violence; its ideology is agronomic. Group B, on the other hand, sees forestry as fundamentally different from agronomy because it employs natural species, and manages a natural environment rather than creating an artificial one. Group B prefers natural reproduction on principle. It worries on biotic as well as economic grounds about the loss of species like chestnut, and the threatened loss of the white pines. It worries about a whole series of secondary forest functions: wildlife, recreation, watersheds, wilderness areas. To my mind, Group B feels the stirrings of an ecological conscience.

In the wildlife field, a parallel cleavage exists. For Group A the basic commodities are sport and meat; the yardsticks of production are ciphers of take in pheasants and trout. Artificial propagation is acceptable as a permanent as well as a temporary recourse—if its unit costs permit. Group B, on the other hand, worries about a whole series of biotic side-issues. What is the cost in predators of producing a game crop? Should we have further recourse to exotics? How can management restore the shrinking species, like prairie grouse, already hopeless as shootable game? How can management restore the threatened rarities, like trumpeter swan and whooping crane? Can management principles be extended to wildflowers? Here again it is clear to me that we have the same A-B cleavage as in forestry.

In the larger field of agriculture I am less competent to speak, but there seem to be somewhat parallel cleavages. Scientific agriculture was actively developing before ecology was born, hence a slower penetration of ecological concepts might be expected. Moreover the farmer, by the very nature of his techniques, must modify the biota more radically than the forester or the wildlife manager. Nevertheless, there are many discontents in agriculture which seem to add up to a new vision of "biotic farming."

Perhaps the most important of these is the new evidence that poundage or tonnage is no measure of the food-value of farm crops; the products of fertile soil may be qualitatively as well as quantitatively superior. We can bolster poundage from depleted soils by pouring on imported fertility, but we are not necessarily bolstering food-value. The possible ultimate ramifications of this idea are so immense that I must leave their exposition to abler pens.

The discontent that labels itself "organic farming," while bearing some of the earmarks of a cult, is nevertheless biotic in its direction, particularly in its insistence on the importance of soil flora and fauna.

The ecological fundamentals of agriculture are just as poorly known to the public as in other fields of land-use. For example, few educated people realize that the marvelous advances in technique made during recent decades are improvements in the pump, rather than the well. Acre for acre, they have barely sufficed to offset the sinking level of fertility.

In all of these cleavages, we see repeated the same basic paradoxes: man the conqueror *versus* man the biotic citizen; science the sharpener of his sword *versus* science the searchlight on his universe; land the slave and servant *versus* land the collective organism. Robinson's injunction to Tristram may well be applied, at this juncture, to *Homo sapiens* as a species in geological time:

Whether you will or not
You are a King, Tristram, for you are one
Of the time-tested few that leave the world,
When they are gone, not the same place it was.
Mark what you leave.

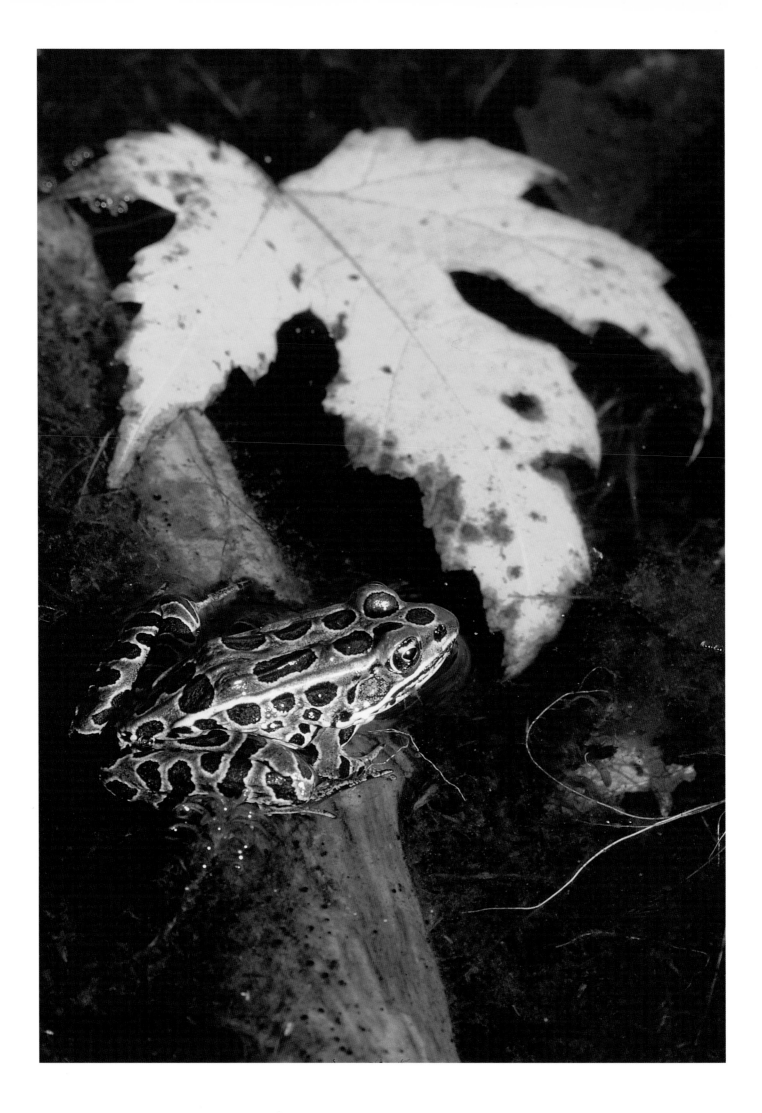

The Outlook

IT IS INCONCEIVABLE TO ME THAT AN ETHICAL RELATION TO LAND can exist without love, respect, and admiration for land, and a high regard for its value. By value, I of course mean something far broader than mere economic value; I mean value in the philosophical sense.

Perhaps the most serious obstacle impeding the evolution of a land ethic is the fact that our educational and economic system is headed away from, rather than toward, an intense consciousness of land. Your true modern is separated from the land by many middlemen, and by innumerable physical gadgets. He has no vital relation to it; to him it is the space between cities on which crops grow. Turn him loose for a day on the land, and if the spot does not happen to be a golf links or a scenic area, he is bored stiff. If crops could be raised by hydroponics instead of farming, it would suit him very well. Synthetic substitutes for wood, leather, wool, and other natural land products suit him better than the originals. In short, land is something he has "outgrown."

Almost equally serious as an obstacle to a land ethic is the attitude of the farmer for whom the land is still an adversary, or a taskmaster that keeps him in slavery. Theoretically, the mechanization of farming ought to cut the farmer's chains, but whether it really does is debatable.

One of the requisites for an ecological comprehension of land is an understanding of ecology, and this is by no means co-extensive with "education"; in fact, much higher education seems deliberately to avoid ecological concepts. An understanding of ecology does not necessarily originate in courses bearing ecological labels; it is quite as likely to be labeled geography, botany, agronomy, history, or economics. This is as it should be, but whatever the label, ecological training is scarce.

The case for a land ethic would appear hopeless but for the minority which is in obvious revolt against these "modern" trends.

The "key-log" which must be moved to release the evolutionary process for an ethic is simply this: quit thinking about decent land-use as solely an economic problem. Examine each question in terms of what is ethically and esthetically right, as well as what is economically expedient. A thing is right when it tends to preserve the integrity, stability, and beauty of the biotic community. It is wrong when it tends otherwise.

Leopard frog, Chapman Lake

It of course goes without saying that economic feasibility limits the tether of what can or cannot be done for land. It always has and it always will. The fallacy the economic determinists have tied around our collective neck, and which we now need to cast off, is the belief that economics determines *all* land-use. This is simply not true. An innumerable host of actions and attitudes, comprising perhaps the bulk of all land relations, is determined by the land-users' tastes and predilections, rather than by his purse. The bulk of all land relations hinges on investments of time, forethought, skill, and faith rather than on investments of cash. As a land-user thinketh, so is he.

I have purposely presented the land ethic as a product of social evolution because nothing so important as an ethic is ever "written." Only the most superficial student of history supposes that Moses "wrote" the Decalogue; it evolved in the minds of a thinking community, and Moses wrote a tentative summary of it for a "seminar." I say tentative because evolution never stops.

The evolution of a land ethic is an intellectual as well as emotional process. Conservation is paved with good intentions which prove to be futile, or even dangerous, because they are devoid of critical understanding either of the land, or of economic land-use. I think it is a truism that as the ethical frontier advances from the individual to the community, its intellectual content increases.

The mechanism of operation is the same for any ethic: social approbation for right actions: social disapproval for wrong actions.

By and large, our present problem is one of attitudes and implements. We are remodeling the Alhambra with a steam-shovel, and we are proud of our yardage. We shall hardly relinquish the shovel, which after all has many good points, but we are in need of gentler and more objective criteria for its successful use.

The farm, winter

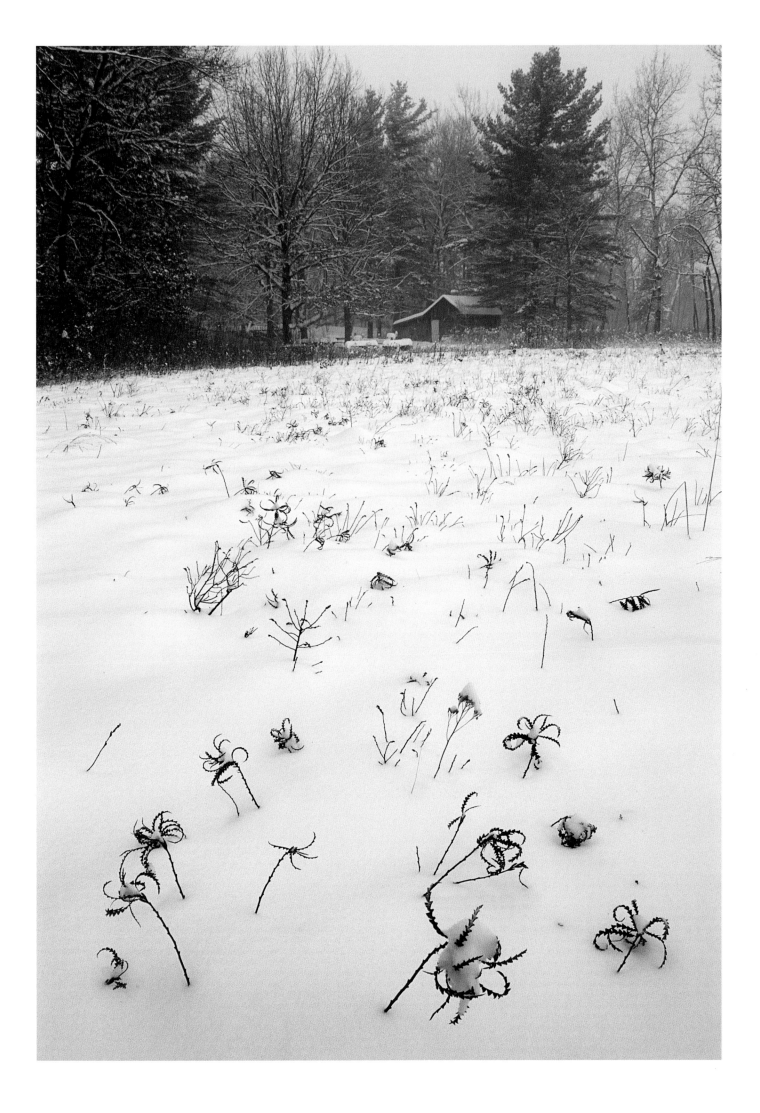

ACKNOWLEDGEMENTS

THE ALDO LEOPOLD FOUNDATION, KENNETH BROWER, AND MICHAEL AND DENISE SEWELL would like to thank Jim Archer, Jeb Barzen, Gary Beeman, Charlie and Nina Leopold Bradley, Russell Calkins, Carol Coyle, Carol Dizack, Brian Dhuey, James and Joan Fedkenheuer, Susan Flader, Peter Ginna, Lisa Hartman, Buddy Huffaker, International Crane Foundation, Mike Jones, Hiroshi and Arlene Kanno, Lynn Kushel, Luna Leopold, Estella Leopold, Carl Leopold, Vernon Lunde, Curt Meine, Jed Meunier, Mike Mossman, Rob Nelson, The New Lab/San Francisco, CA, Nikon, Inc., Shane Overton, William and Brian Pierce, Sid Poe, Robin Rider, Anne Ross, Galen Rowell, Sand County Foundation, Bernard Schermetzler, Norbert and Ruth Schmitz, Teresa Searock, Ted and Jennifer Stanley, Steve Swenson, Frank and Colleen Terbilcox, Terry Family Foundation, Janet Vail, and Mark Vladick for their assistance in making this book possible.

THE ALDO LEOPOLD FOUNDATION

BUILDING UPON THE VISION Aldo Leopold set forth in *A Sand County Almanac* and other works, the Aldo Leopold Foundation strives to promote the care of natural resources and foster an ethical relationship between people and land.

Demonstrating this ethic on the original Leopold Family Farm outside Baraboo, Wisconsin, the Foundation seeks to restore the ecological health and integrity of the prairie, oak savanna, woodland, and riparian communities once abundant in this area. Working closely with neighbor and other private landowners, Foundation staff, interns, and volunteers share their stewardship expertise throughout the region to save and restore "every cog and wheel," so that the land retains its capacity for self-renewal.

Field trips for students and adults to the forests, wetlands, and prairies surrounding the Leopold Shack provide an outdoor classroom for exploring ecological relationships. The Foundation also sponsors seminars, workshops, and special education programs to provide private landowners and public land managers with the tools they need to achieve their own Land Ethic.

Founded in 1982 by the children of Aldo Leopold, the Foundation depends on a strong and growing membership to support its ongoing work toward developing a conservation ethic in the minds and actions of our society. For more information or to become a member, please contact:

The Aldo Leopold Foundation
P.O. Box 77, Baraboo, WI 53913
(608) 355-0279
www.aldoleopold.org

One hundred and twenty acres,

of my worldly domain.   But the Co

books
looks at his record, before nine o'clock

is the question here at issue.

Books or no books, it is a fact, [up]

that at daybreak I am the sole [o]

over, and that solitude, (no long)

extends on every hand
~~stretches~~ as far as the deer can [s]

able to plcain.

Like other great landowners,

about rents, but very punctilious